CREATION

ACTS • FACTS • IMPACTS

Clive Thomson
292 North Rd
Bedford Mass

A compilation of articles of permanent interest from
ICR ACTS & FACTS, Vol. I, No. 1, to Vol. II, No.
9, plus ICR "Impact Series", Numbers 1 through 9.

Edited by

Henry M. Morris, Ph.D.,
Duane T. Gish, Ph.D.,
George M. Hillestad

Please return

1st Printing, January 1974
2nd Printing, May 1974

CONTENTS

INTRODUCTION

The I.C.R. monthly publication ACTS AND FACTS, together with the "Impact" article enclosed with each issue, has truly been making an *impact* on many people, judging from the response we receive after each mail-out. The ACTS AND FACTS is sent free-of-charge each month to all who request to be on our mailing list, and hundreds of names are added every month.

Requests for back copies of ACTS AND FACTS, received from readers who have just begun receiving it, are becoming more numerous all the time. We have had to reprint back issues in large numbers to meet these requests.

This book is a compilation of all these back issues, from the first one in June, 1972, through the issue of December, 1973. All the articles of continuing interest, especially each article in the "Impact" Series, have been incorporated. The only items deleted are announcements which were of current interest at the time (speaking schedules, etc.) but which are out-of-date now. First the news articles appear, arranged chronologically, and then the "Impact" articles, also in chronological sequence.

The book, hopefully, will meet the continuing need for back copies of ACTS AND FACTS requested by new readers. Perhaps, even more, it will serve as a documentary on the creationist revival we believe our nation is beginning to experience. It should also make a fascinating gift book for young people and for others who are interested (or who need to be interested) in these issues.

We anticipate that a similar compilation will be issued in book form annually in the future. We are very grateful for the high reader interest in our ACTS AND FACTS, which has made such a publication necessary. We trust its ministry will be multiplied many fold as it goes out again in this form.

Henry M. Morris
Director, Institute for Creation Research

CREATION HITS THE CAMPUS

Reverberations are still being felt on the campuses of the University of California, Davis, due to a series of seminars featuring Dr. Henry Morris, Director of the Institute for Creation Research, and Dr. Duane T. Gish, its Associate Director.

Last fall Dr. Morris presented several evening seminars at the University of Hawaii and lectured to numerous classes during the day. Dr. Morris established an excellent rapport with the students and faculty and his lectures on a series of creation science subjects were surprisingly well received. A poll of students, in one class, by the professor before and after Dr. Morris' lecture to the class showed a considerable shift of opinion away from evolution and to the creation position. Some faculty members expressed interest in joining the Creation Research Society, a 400-member creation-scientist association of which Dr. Morris is president.

Last fall Dr. Gish presented a two-day seminar in the Sacramento area. Those in the audience included students from the University of California at Davis, an 18,000 student university. One of the students gave copies of Dr. Gish's articles and tapes of his lectures to his biology professor. Having been, as he put it later, "brainwashed on the subject of evolution," the professor was amazed at the mass of scientific evidence exposing weaknesses and fallacies in evolution theory. He decided to devote one of his special study courses to the subject of creation/evolution.

This course had 40 students enrolled, about equally divided between the creation and evolution positions. They were given copies of Dr. Gish's publications as a starter and asked to spend the term investigating various aspects of the creation/evolution problem. The final class session of several hours duration was to be devoted to the reports by the students. Dr. Gish was asked to come to help interpret and defend the creationist position, while the world-famous evolutionist, Dr. G. Ledyard Stebbins, a faculty member at Davis, was to be present to defend the evolutionist position.

Facilities necessarily limited attendance at the reporting session by the students and opportunity for debate between Dr. Gish and Dr. Stebbins was also limited. An evening lecture offered a vastly greater opportunity. One of the reporters on the student newspaper, the *Aggie*, was a Christian and had heard Dr. Gish's lectures in Sacramento. The day of Dr. Gish's evening seminar on the campus, she published a full-page article in the Aggie headlined, "Have You Been Brainwashed on Evolution?" The article presented a summary of Dr. Gish's Sacramento lectures and challenged students and faculty to hear his evening lecture. The result was astounding.

The lecture hall, which seated 800, was packed to capacity, with students sitting in the aisles and doorways and on the floor in the front of the auditorium. In the audience were Dr. Stebbins and other faculty members. Dr. Gish presented the creation model, the evolution model, the predictions based on each model, and then proceeded to show that the actual evidence was much more in accord with creation than evolution. At the close of the lecture the audience responded with a prolonged ovation. This lecture was apparently like a breath of fresh air to these students who suddenly realized that they had been subjected to a process of one-sided indoctrination by many of their teachers.

What followed essentially amounted to a 2½-hour debate between Dr. Gish and Dr. Stebbins and his fellow evolutionists on the faculty. Dr. Stebbins and his colleagues were repeatedly forced to offer subsidiary hypotheses in attempts to cover up fallacies and weaknesses in the evolution theory which had been exposed by Dr. Gish. The campus was buzzing the next day with many groups discussing the events of the previous evening. The next edition of the student newspaper carried an excellent summary of Dr. Gish's lecture and a reply by Dr. Stebbins. Dr. Gish was subsequently permitted to publish a rebuttal to Dr. Stebbins' article.

Some weeks later, Dr. Morris was invited to lecture on the Davis campus. The case for creation was presented in Dr. Morris' inimitable fashion, this time stressing the thermodynamic approach. Once again Dr. Stebbins rose to defend the evolution theory, but did not attempt to deal with any of the specific arguments. Instead, he merely delivered an emotional defense of himself and other evolutionists against an inferred identification with racism.

These debates amply demonstrated that creation scientists need not yield an inch when eyeball-to-eyeball with the world's leading evolutionists. The scientific case for creation is, indeed, eminently sound. The response by students on the secular campuses to these messages is astoundingly warm and appreciative. A much wider acceptance for the creation cause is being hindered because of limited resources at our disposal.

Dr. Gish and Dr. Morris have also spoken in recent months to student and faculty groups at such secular colleges and universities as Florida Technological University (where Dr. Morris was invited as one of the speakers on the Graduate Colloquium series), Long Beach College, University of California-Irvine, University of Alberta, University of Saskatchewan, Drury College, San Fernando State College, Regina University, University of Manitoba, San Diego State University and others.

To these may be added meetings at many Christian colleges, including Tennessee Temple, Multnomah in Portland, Baptist Bible College (Springfield, Mo.), Biola, Los Angeles Baptist College, and many others. We are convinced that a creationist ministry to higher education is of vital importance and are glad for all such opportunities.

THE MATHEMATICAL IMPOSSIBILITY
OF EVOLUTION

According to the accepted theory of evolution today, the sole mechanism for producing evolution is that of random mutation and natural selection. Mutations are *random* changes in genetic systems. Natural selection is considered by evolutionists to be a sort of sieve which retains the "good" mutations and allows the others to pass away.

Now random changes in ordered systems almost always will decrease the amount of order in those systems, and therefore, nearly all mutations are harmful to the organisms which experience them. Nevertheless, the evolutionist insists that each complex organism in the world today has arisen by a long string of gradually-accumulated, good mutations preserved by natural selection.

No one has ever actually *observed* a genuine mutation occurring in the natural environment which was beneficial, and therefore, retained by the selection process. For some reason, however, the idea has a certain persuasive quality about it and seems eminently reasonable to many people — until it is examined *quantitatively*, that is!

For example, consider a very simple organism composed of only 200 integrated and functioning parts, and the problem of deriving that organism by this type of process. Obviously, the organism must have started with only one part and then gradually built itself up over many generations into its 200-part organization. The developing organism, at each successive stage, must itself be integrated and functioning in its environment in order to survive until the next stage. Each successive stage, of course, becomes less likely than the preceding one, since it is far easier for a complex system to break down then to build itself up. A four-component integrated system can more easily mutate into a three-component system (or even a four-component non-functioning system) than into a five-component integrated system. If, at any step in the chain, the system mutates backward or downward, then it is either destroyed altogether or else moves backward.

Therefore, the successful production of a 200-component functioning organism requires, *at least*, 200 successive, successful mutations, each of which is highly unlikely. Even evolutionists recognize that true mutations are very rare, and beneficial mutations are *extremely* rare — not more than one out of a thousand mutations are beneficial, at the very most.

But let us give the evolutionist the benefit of every consideration. Assume that, at each mutational step, there is equally as much chance for it to be good as bad. Thus, the probability for the success of each mutation is assumed to be one out of two, or one-half. Elementary statistical theory shows that the probability of 200 successive mutations being successful is then $(1/2)^{200}$, or one chance out of 10^{60}. The number 10^{60}, if written out, would be "one" followed by sixty "zeros." In other words, the chance that a 200-component organism could be formed by mutation and natural selection is less than one chance out of a trillion, trillion, trillion, trillion, trillion! Lest anyone think that a 200-part system is unreasonably complex, it should be noted that even a one-celled plant or animal may have millions of molecular "parts."

The evolutionist might react by saying that even though any one such mutating organism might not be successful, surely some around the world would be, especially in the 10 billion years (or 10^{18} seconds) of assumed earth history. Therefore, let us imagine that every one of the earth's 10^{14} square feet of surface harbors a billion (i.e. 10^9) mutating systems and that each mutation requires one-half second (actually it would take far more time than this). Each system can thus go through its 200 mutations in 100 seconds and then, if it is unsuccessful, start over for a new try. In 10^{18} seconds, there can, therefore, be $10^{18}/10^2$, or 10^{16}, trials by each mutating system. Multiplying all these numbers together, there would be a total possible number of attempts to develop a 200-component system equal to $10^{14}(10^9)$ (10^{16}), or 10^{39} attempts. Since the probability against the success of any one of them is 10^{60}, it is obvious that the probability just one of these 10^{39} attempts might be successful is only one out of $10^{60}/10^{39}$, or 10^{21}.

All of this means that the chance that any kind of a 200-component integrated functioning organism could be developed by mutation and natural selection just once, anywhere in the world, in all the assumed expanse of geologic time, is less than one chance out of a billion trillion. What possible conclusion, therefore, can we derive from such considerations as this except that evolution by mutation and natural selection is mathematically and logically indefensible!

Dr. Gish lecturing at Summer Institute on Scientific Creationism.

MT. ARARAT EXPEDITION 1972

Probably the most extensive photographic survey of the higher elevations of Mount Ararat ever obtained was one of the accomplishments of the 1972 ICR Summer Expedition. In search of Noah's Ark, the team of five men, led by John Morris, spent a total of three summer weeks on the forbidding mountain slopes. Though the explorers did not discover the location of the Ark on this expedition, the ICR team was able to thoroughly explore one of the regions of its probable location. On several occasions, while in the dangerous Ahora Gorge, the exploration, except for the miraculous deliverance of the Lord, could have cost the team members their lives.

Because their explorations were more thorough and extensive than former Mount Ararat expeditions, the ICR team was able to narrow down considerably the regions of future search. However, as they were beginning a climb into another exploration area, gun-carrying Kurdish bandits robbed the team of all their equipment, forcing a temporary abandonment of the expedition.

Despite these setbacks, the Institute for Creation Research hopes to be able to continue the exploratory project next summer, believing prospects are brighter for the actual discovery of Noah's Ark. These expeditions, however, are obviously costly and depend on the continued receipt of special gifts designated for this endeavor.

The project director, John Morris, a young civil engineer and son of Dr. Henry M. Morris, is available for speaking engagements in churches and other organizations interested in this fascinating archaeological adventure. With a beautiful and breathtaking slide presentation of previously unexplored regions of Mount Ararat, the young explorer tells his story of God's miraculous guidance and protection in otherwise impossible situations. Churches and interested groups wishing to hear this thrilling story should contact the Institute for Creation Research, 2716 Madison Avenue, San Diego, California 92116.

DIRECTOR'S COLUMN
Henry M. Morris, Ph.D.

One of the most thrilling aspects of the study of the Genesis Flood to me has always been the story of Noah himself. The Scriptures speak of "giants in the earth in those days" (Genesis 6:4) and these were not only giants in physical stature but giants in wickedness — "the earth also was corrupt before God, and the earth was filled with violence" (Genesis 6:11).

But Noah was also a giant — a *spiritual* giant! "Noah was a just man and perfect in his generations, and Noah walked with God" (Genesis 6:9).

Christ said that the last days before His coming would be like Noah's days. As we confront the secularized world of our generation, we can profit much by studying and emulating Noah's example in his generation. Consider the following:

1. First of all, "Noah found grace in the eyes of the Lord" (Genesis 6:8). This is the first mention of *grace* in the Bible. Before anyone can expect to be used by God in this generation, as in that generation, he must first be the recipient of God's saving grace, entering into the family of God through faith in the Saviour, Jesus Christ.

2. Twice it is stated (Genesis 6:22; 7:5) that "Noah did according to *all* that God commanded him." When God's Word directed him to build an immense boat, he proceeded to build it according to the exact instruction; when the Word told him to take two of every kind of land animal into the boat, that he did. By any measure of the science and experience of his day, such actions were altogether foolish, but Noah believed and obeyed God's Word. In our day, we are ill-advised if we try to pick and choose among the Scriptures, believing only those portions that seem acceptable to current human experience and scientific philosophy. We must live today "by *every* word of God" if we are to win victory over the devil (Luke 4:4).

3. Noah had to confront the uniformitarians of his day, as

10

we do in ours. The meteorologists had never seen rain at all (Genesis 2:5) and the hydrologists knew nothing of even a local flood, let alone a world-wide flood. The geologists knew where to find metals and precious stones (Genesis 2:12), but it is unlikely they had even seen any fossils or earth movements. Nevertheless, Noah believed and preached God's Word, though his "model" of coming catastrophism was so contrary to common scientific experience that he never gained any followers. He, "being warned of God of things not seen as yet" (Hebrews 11:7), simply continued to pattern his preaching and practice after God's precepts. And so should we.

4. Though Noah gained few (none, so far as the record goes) converts in the world, his faithfulness did at least result in the saving of his own household. "Come thou and all thy house into the ark: for thee have I seen righteous before me in this generation" (Genesis 7:1). "He prepared an ark to the saving of his house" Hebrews 11:7). Christian parents today are rightly exercised about the ungodly influences of the world — especially the educational system and the media of communication — on their own children. The easy way is to drift, to compromise, to seek worldly advantage and recognition for them. But this is the way to lose them! The way to save them is, like Noah, to stand strong, to preach righteousness, to pray much, to work hard, to believe and obey God's Word in all its fullness and simplicity.

Here at the Institute for Creation Research we are trying, as God's grace enables, to provide a service which will help people to stand true to God's Word in this generation — and also especially to help our own young people (we are all parents too!) "overcome the wicked one" (I John 2:13). God bless you as you stand with us.

CREATIONISM BREAKTHROUGH

Creation scientists will have a unique opportunity to present the scientific case for special creation before 1,000 or more biology teachers at the 1972 National Convention of the National Association of Biology Teachers (NABT) to be held in San Francisco this fall. This annual meeting of the nation's biology teachers will be held at the Hilton Hotel, Thursday through Saturday, October 26-28.

Upon learning that the theme of the 1972 convention was to be "Biology and Evolution," Dr. Gish wrote to the program chairman and suggested that omission of the creationist's interpretation of biology and origins would be a serious oversight at a meeting devoted to the above theme. He requested that at least half a day be reserved for a symposium presenting the creationist's viewpoint. The program committee instead agreed to schedule a two-hour "mini-symposium" for the creationist's interpretation of origins.

As part of this mini-symposium, Dr. John N. Moore, professor at Michigan State, managing editor of the Creation Research Society Quarterly and member of the Advisory Council of the Institute for Creation Research, will present a paper entitled, "Evolution, Creation, and the Scientific Method." Dr. Gish will present a paper, "Evolution, Creation, and the Historical Evidence," as the second part of the mini-symposium. This symposium is scheduled to begin at 1:00 p.m. on Friday afternoon.

A regular paper session will follow the mini-symposium. During this session, Dr. George Howe, Chairman of the Science Division at Los Angeles Baptist College and editor of the Creation Research Society Quarterly, will present a paper entitled, "Homology, Analogy, and Innovative Teaching." Dr. Howe will show that the homologies and analogies seen in biology can be explained more readily and satisfactorily within the creation concept than within the concept of evolution. Dr. Gish will present a paper entitled, "A Critique of Speculations and Experiments Related to Theories on the Origin of Life."

Dr. Gish will expose the fallacies and weaknesses in such speculations and experiments, claiming that the origin of life without the intervention of a Creator would have been impossible.

It is suspected that the choice of the theme "Biology and Evolution" for this year's convention came as a reaction to the impact creationists have been making in the last few years in educational and scientific circles. Evolutionists are especially chagrined at the 1969 decision of the California State Board of Education that henceforth evolution must be taught as only a theory and that creation must also be taught. Members of the Creation Research Society played a prominent role in securing this decision, and as a result received attention in scientific journals throughout the world. Creation scientists have presented papers before academic and scientific circles in the last few years that have created a considerable stir.

The program committee of the National Association of Biology Teachers has scheduled some of the nation's most prominent evolutionists for the 1972 convention. Included are Dr. G. Ledyard Stebbins, whom Dr. Gish debated earlier this year (see Acts and Facts, Vol. 1, No. 1), and Dr. Theodosius Dobzhansky, both world-famous evolutionists. The title of Dr. Dobzhansky's address will be, "Nothing in Biology Makes Sense Except in the Light of Evolution." This is, of course, totally absurd. Dr. Gish was tempted to title his talk, "Nothing in Evolution Makes Sense in the Light of Biology!" In any case, Dr. Dobzhansky's address can be expected to be a propaganda blast aimed in the direction of creationists.

Dr. Bentley Glass, a well-known evolutionist, is scheduled to appear with two other biologists on Saturday morning in a mini-symposium on "Evolution and the Courts." Creationists will be present in the audience prepared to comment on provisions of the U.S. Constitution, opinions of U.S. Supreme Court justices, and various legal opinions and rulings which prohibit the teaching of, or favoritism toward, *any* philosophical view. Such rulings definitely prohibit the teaching of evolution as fact or restricting the teaching of origins to any single view to the exclusion of all others. Most evolutionists, including Glass, insist that teaching in the public schools be restricted to the theory of evolution and are attempting to obtain a reversal of the ruling of the California State Board of Education mentioned earlier.

Last year Dr. John Moore and Dr. Gish had been invited to appear on a panel at the 1971 National Convention of the National Association of Biology Teachers to discuss the subject of "Evolution and the Law." Before the convention, however, the panel was canceled due to pressure from prominent evolutionists in the NABT. This year the symposium on "Evolution and the Courts" will be restricted to participation by Dr. Bentley Glass and other evolutionists. Any participation by creationists will have to come from the floor. The loading of this year's panel with evolutionists and the exclusion of creationists will, of course, lead to a one-sided presentation.

The 1972 convention of the NABT features five general sessions and five mini-symposia. Creationists have been allotted none of the general sessions and only one of the mini-symposia. This, of course, does not even approach a balanced presentation, but then we must recognize that the creationist viewpoint is the minority viewpoint. The allocation of a portion of the program of a national meeting of biology teachers for a presentation of the creationist viewpoint is a breakthrough of considerable magnitude for which we can all be grateful. We believe that this occasion will aid in opening up even greater opportunities for creationists in the future.

PETROLEUM IN MINUTES
COAL IN HOURS
Duane T. Gish, Ph.D.

Theories concerning the formation of coal based on the assumptions of uniformitarian geologists generally postulate that coal was formed from trees and other vegetable matter growing in extensive peat bogs found in tropical areas. It is assumed that dead organic material accumulated in these forests for thousands to many tens of thousands of years, depending on the thickness of the seam, before this material was buried by a rise in the level of nearby seas. Compression under a vast weight of overlying sediment through millions of years resulted in the coal deposits found today, it is said.

This *in situ* theory, or autochthonous theory as it is called, is preferred by most evolutionary geologists. There are some geologists who, even though committed to the evolutionary hypothesis and geological ages, argue that the evidence indicates that the organic material which contributed to the formation of the coal did not grow where the coal is now found, but was deposited there by water transport. They have proposed that this plant material was carried by rivers into lakes or estuaries where it was buried. This is known as the allochthonous theory of coal formation.

The allochthonous or transport theory of coal formation is advocated by catastrophist geologists who believe that the earth and the life on it were the result of a recent creation rather than the product of evolutionary changes through immense stretches of geologic time. Of the 20th Century catastrophists, George McCready Price (*The New Geology*, 1923) was the pioneer. John C. Whitcomb and Henry M. Morris (*The Genesis Flood*, 1964) inspired a

15

great modern revival in creationist catastrophism. Price and Whitcomb and Morris maintained that the great Noahic Flood accounted for the transport and sudden burial of the vast amounts of vegetal material required for the formation of the coal seams found in the earth today.

Melvin Cook (*Prehistory and Earth Models*, 1966) has also advocated a catastrophic allochthonous (transport) process for the burial and conversion of the plant material into coal. His ice cap model of continental drift postulates sudden thrusting and deep vegetal burial under variable loads of strata.

It has generally been supposed by uniformitarian geologists that oil and gas were generated largely from marine type organisms during compaction of a sedimentary basin. Again it is asserted that geologic ages were required for its formation, following which the oil collected in traps.

The models of creation catastrophists, such as those of Whitcomb and Morris and of Cook, on the other hand, account for the conversion of marine or vegetal matter into oil and gas in a relatively short time. As these authors point out (Cook has presented an especially well-documented case), the time required to convert cellulosic matter into coal, and cellulosic or marine organic matter into oil and gas, is determined by the temperature and pressure. The process would be quite rapid at the high temperatures and pressures generated by a combination of burial and friction which would have resulted from the flooding and earth movements postulated in their models.

It has now been experimentally demonstrated that *cellulosic (plant derived) material, such as garbage or manure, can be converted into a good grade of petroleum in 20 minutes.* In other experiments, *wood or other cellulosic material was converted into coal or coal-like products in a matter of hours.* These experiments conclusively demonstrate that the formation of coal and oil did not necessarily require millions of years or even thousands of years to form, but that such products could have formed easily within the relatively short time since the Flood.

The Formation of Oil

The experiments of Bureau of Mines scientists in which cow manure was converted to petroleum are described in Chemical and Engineering News, May 29, 1972, p. 14. The process could also utilize other cellulosic materials such as wood, bark, corn husks, rice hulls, wheat straw, sewage, sludge, and garbage. Two methods were used. In the first method a pyrolytic method, the material was heated under pressure in the presence of steam and carbon monoxide, with or without a catalyst.

In the first method, manure or other material was heated in a closed system at 900° centigrade (1652° Fahreneit) for about six hours. The products were gas, oil, and solids, all of which can be used for fuel. This experiment probably has less relevancy to the formation of oil and gas in the earth because of the very high temperature used. The same results might be obtained, however, with the non-cellulosic material of marine organisms at a much lower temperature by extending the heating period to days, weeks, or months.

In the second method, the manure was heated at 380°C (716°F), at 2000 to 5000 p.s.i. for 20 minutes in the presence of carbon monoxide and steam. the product was a heavy oil of excellent heating quality. The yield was about three barrels of oil per ton of manure.

As Cook has pointed out, protoplasm and chlorophyll are present in marine organisms. These components readily decompose, so there should be no difficulty in getting the reaction started, even at relatively low temperatures, during the conversion of these organisms to gas and oil. The heat generated by compression, the increase in temperature with depth, and the heat generated by friction of crustal thrusting caused by the tremendous cataclysmic burial and earth movements which occurred at the time of the Flood would have caused the temperature to rise sufficiently to initiate the exothermic reaction (heat is given off during this chemical reaction). The reaction would then, under the temperature and pressure generated, have proceeded to completion. The nature of the products would have been determined by the particular conditions of temperature and pressure under which these products formed.

The Formation of Coal

The formation of coal from woody or other cellulosic material, in a very short time, was demonstrated by experiments performed by Dr. George R. Hill of the College of Mines and Mineral Industries of the University of Utah. His report may be found in Chem Tech, May, 1972, p. 296.

In these experiments the material was heated under high confining pressures. The reaction was exothermic, and had a negative pressure coefficient, that is, the lower the pressure the lower the temperature required to initiate the reaction. Some special features of Dr. Hill's experimental results have very important implications for the formation of coal under the catastrophic conditions proposed by flood geologists, or by Melvin Cook with his ice cap model of continental drift, which would have occurred catastrophically shortly after the time of the Flood.

Dr. Hill found that when the rate of heating was increased from 0.5°C per minute to 5°C per minute, a dramatic temperature rise occurred in the temperature range of 220° to 260°C. This sudden rise in temperature, which amounted to 200° to 400°, indicated the onset of a highly exothermic reaction. Properties of the products were similar to those found in anthracite and low volatile bituminous coals.

The significance of these results with reference to the Flood and other catastrophic models is evident from Dr. Hill's remarks. He stated that, "These observations suggest that in their formation, high rank coals, i.e., anthracite and low volatile bituminous, which contain large concentrations of multi-ring carbon-hydrogen structures, were probably subjected to high temperature at some stage in their history.

A possible mechanism for formation of these high rank coals could have been a short time, rapid heating event."

Here, then, is experimental evidence that these coals may not only have formed rapidly, but that *their formation may have required catastrophic short time events.* Such events would be required to generate the rapid rise in temperature which apparently is necessary for the initiation of the highly exothermic reaction involved in the production of these coals. The tremendous catastrophic earth movements associated with the "breaking up of the great deep" (Gen. 7:11) during the Noahic Flood, or with the catastrophic continental breakup proposed by Cook, would provide the mechanism necessary to produce such conditions.

On the other hand, the uniformitarian geological model, the evolutionary model postulating billions of years for the age of the earth and geological processes proceeding at rates visible today, has no mechanism for generating such conditions, certainly not on the worldwide scale required. According to presently accepted theories of evolutionary geologists on mountain building and continental drift, these processes were very slow, requiring tens of millions of years. Such processes would thus have resulted in very slow, gradual change and could not have provided the short time, rapid heating event indicated by Dr. Hill as necessary.

We must emphasize that the evidence discussed in this article does not prove that oil and coal were produced by a catastrophic event such as the Flood. Science has no way of ever proving anything that has occurred in the past. Such evidence is persuasive evidence in support of Flood geology, however, and certainly does prove that millions of years were not necessary for the formation of these products, but that they could have formed in an extremely short time, geologically speaking.

THE LIBERATING MESSAGE OF CREATION

The good news of a perfect, finished, recent creation often breaks in on the heart of a believer like a breath of clear air. We hear this testimony over and over again from Christians who once were uncertain in their spiritual convictions and vacillating in their testimonies, not quite sure whether they could really believe what God has said. When suddenly they learned with certainty that the Bible is confirmed by all genuine science and can be confidently trusted in all things, it was nothing less than release from bondage.

God is to them no more a God of the long-ago and far-away, but a God who is near, a very-present help, not far from every one of us. The world no longer is a decadent remnant of vast aeons of grinding struggle and chance mutation, but is a beautiful, friendly world, everywhere bearing witness to the One who "did good, and gave us rain from heaven, and fruitful seasons, filling our hearts with food and gladness" (Acts 14:17).

It may be true, of course, that one who believes in a real creation will encounter a measure of opposition and ridicule, but that is nothing — not when compared with the wonderful freedom of knowing that God's Word and God's World are both true and are good for time and eternity. God is really *there*! And He *created* us — for Himself!

Even the sorrows of the world become understandable, and therefore bearable. God indeed has cursed the ground, but even that was "for man's sake" (Genesis 3:17). God so loved the world that He could not leave man to wander unhindered forever, and so He uses the discipline of suffering and the fear of death to show man his need of salvation.

And then — to realize that the same powerful God who created him is the gracious Saviour who loved him and died for him — to really realize *that* is immediately to bow in humble adoration and there proclaim: "My God, how great thou art!"

Only the one who knows the Lord Jesus Christ as Creator and Sustainer of all things (Colossians 1:16, 17), sensing His eternal purpose and His continued providential care for His wounded creation, can begin to comprehend the majesty and magnitude of the peace He made "with the blood of His cross, by Him to reconcile all things unto Himself" (Colossians 1:20), and thus know Him with real thanksgiving as Saviour and Lord.

This is high freedom — freedom not merely from the guilt of sin, but also freedom to enjoy God's world, freedom from the need to compromise with man's errant philosophies, freedom from lingering doubts as to the reality of those things we profess to believe, freedom from fear lest God is unable to perform what He has promised. "If the Son therefore shall make you free, ye shall be free indeed" (John 8:36).

November is the month of Thanksgiving. "Thanks be unto God for His unspeakable gift" (II Corinthians 9:15).

OUT OF THE MAILBAG

"At last — another approach — a major change of view that shows light."   R.B.S., California

"I am so glad God has led capable men to lead in this line of study. I believe evolution is the best tool Satan can use to destroy the minds of young people."

M.A.S., Louisiana

"May God bless all your staff and the efforts being made to teach about a God-created universe."

R.A.E., Tennessee

"I . . . am thrilled and blessed beyond description with the way you have been able to uphold the honor of God on those campuses mentioned."   M.A.C., MD, Maryland

1972 NABT CONVENTION
CREATION vs. EVOLUTION!

The announced theme of the 1972 annual convention of the National Association of Biology Teachers, held in San Francisco, October 26-28, was "Biology and Evolution." Before the first speaker was half way through his address, however, it became evident that the real theme of the convention was "Shoot down the creationists!"

The first speaker on the program was Dr. Theodosius Dobzhansky, famous evolutionist, and for many years Professor of Genetics at Columbia University. The title of his talk, given before an audience of about 1,200, was "Nothing in Biology Makes Sense Except in the Light of Evolution" (we were tempted to change the title of our talk to "Nothing in Evolution Makes Sense in the Light of Biology!"). Dobzhansky's talk actually was a polemic against the creationists (he refused to call them creationists, but insisted that they be called "anti-evolutionists"). He repeatedly referred to "anti-evolutionists" in a derogatory fashion. Dobzhansky even accused the creationists of blasphemy against God! He claimed that creationists in effect accuse God of deception when they say He did not use evolution when He has given us so much evidence that He did! That is a ridiculous statement, of course, and reveals the shallow thinking of evolutionists like Dobzhansky. Not only did God provide us an abundance of evidence that He used special creation and not evolution, but He plainly told us so in Genesis!

Dobzhansky finally got around to listing some of the evidences he claimed supported evolution rather than creation. Creationists were dumbfounded to hear him list the idea of embryological recapitulation as one of the evidences of evolution (this is the idea that the human embryo recapitulates its "evolutionary history," resembling its evolutionary ancestors at various stages of its development). Not only has this theory been thoroughly disproved, and is spurned by most leading evolutionists, but it is totally bankrupt intellectually. It was excusable to believe in a flat earth centuries ago, but it is totally inexcusable for a geneticist of Dobzhansky's stature to endorse this false theory in this age. Not only do modern embryologists *know* it isn't true, but the science of genetics has demonstrated that it *could not* be true.

Dobzhansky stated during his address that evolution was purposeless, directionless, and had no fore-ordained goal. But then he identified himself as both an evolutionist and a creationist! What kind of a "creator" is this? — a creator so inept that he had no control over his creation! Surely not the God of Scripture!

Toward the close of his talk, Dobzhansky accused creationists of expertly and deliberately misusing the evidence to support their position and to refute evolution. During the discussion period which followed Dobzhansky's speech, Dr. Gish was the first to obtain the floor. He strongly protested Dobzhansky's charge of deception on the part of creationists and asked those in the audience to withhold judgment until they could hear the creationists' presentation the following day, at which time copies of the papers to be given by the creationists, fully documented in every respect, would be distributed.

At the noon luncheon, Dr. G. Ledyard Stebbins, another world-famous evolutionist whom Dr. Gish had debated at the University of California, Davis, earlier this year, gave an address entitled "Evolution of Design." Stebbins also frequently loosed verbal blasts at "anti-evolutionists." He claimed that there was no real design or purpose in nature, but only apparent design or purpose which resulted from blind and purposeless forces of evolution. In spite of an obvious atheistic approach to his interpretation of nature, Stebbins also claimed to be both an evolutionist and a creationist! What kind of a creator would create without design and purpose? How could there be a creation and all this apparent design and purpose in nature without the Creator being responsible? Dobzhansky and Stebbins are not creationists. They are atheistic evolutionists. Apparently they believe a combination of evolution and a counterfeit creationism will win more support than frank atheistic evolutionism.

Another one of the principal speakers was Dr. Sherwood Washburn, professor at the University of California, Berkeley, who spoke on "Human Evolution." Washburn stated that the fossil record related to man was so scanty that it could not be used to trace his origin. He said that this evidence was so poor that it could be used to support almost any theory. We agree. The known fossil record offers no basis whatever for postulating the origin of man from lower animals.

Washburn believes that the way to determine which of the extant apes is man's nearest relative is to compare the biochemistry of man to the biochemistry of chimpanzees, gorillas, baboons, monkeys, and other anthropoids. When this is done, it turns out that the biochemistry of man is more similar to that of the chimpanzee than to that of any of the other apes. Therefore, Washburn claims, man is more closely related to chimpanzees than to the gorilla, monkey, etc.

Washburn showed an old movie still of a chimpanzee and Dorothy Lamour. The chimpanzee had been coached to assume a pose similar to the actress, with legs crossed, etc. Washburn claimed that, after all, there was very little difference between a chimpanzee and a human. Actually, a primatologist can easily distinguish every bone in an ape from the corresponding bone in a human. We wanted to say to Dr. Washburn that we would agree with his assessment that there is very little difference between a chimpanzee and a human . . . the day he would be willing to take the chimp and give the other fellow Dorothy Lamour!

The opportunity for the creationists finally came on Friday afternoon. Dr. John N. Moore, of Michigan State University, and Dr. Gish were scheduled to present a symposium on the creationist interpretation of origins. Probably the largest crowd at the convention, nearly 1,500 biology teachers, crowded into the lecture hall to hear Moore and Gish.

24

Dr. Moore presented a paper entitled "Creation, Evolution, and the Scientific Method." The thrust of Dr. Moore's paper was that evolutionists use evidence for trivial changes as proof for evolution which would actually have involved changes of tremendous proportions seen nowhere in nature today, or in the fossil record of the past. All of the evidence for evolution is purely circumstantial, and, furthermore, this evidence is more readily explainable by creation than evolution. Evolutionists are guilty of confusion of terms, because they do not have a proper understanding of the scientific method.

Dr. Gish presented a paper on "Creation, Evolution, and the Historical Evidence." Dr. Gish pointed out that since neither creation nor evolution has actually been observed, nor can either be tested experimentally, the best way to evaluate these two opposing views is on the basis of the historical evidence, that is, the fossil record. He compared the creation model to the evolution model, the predictions concerning the fossil record based on each model, and then proceeded to show that the actual fossil record contradicts the predictions of the evolution model, but agrees remarkably well with the creation model.

After the completion of these two talks, there were dozens of people who wanted to ask questions. Moore and Gish, as they had been requested by the program committee, had carefully limited their talks to 40 minutes each in order to allow 25 minutes for questions and answers. To their utter amazement, the symposium Chairman, Dr. Lawrence Cory, of St. Mary's College, stating that he had been instructed to give a rebuttal to the creationist position, used almost 15 minutes of the question and answer period for his personal attempt to refute the evidence presented by Moore and Gish. Such action by a chairman is not only totally without precedent at a scientific meeting, but was most unethical. This portion of the program had been set aside for a presentation of the creationist interpretation of origins, not the evolutionary view. Cory's presentation actually aided the creationist cause because he is a poor speaker,

25

and what he had to say wasn't worth saying anyhow! The symposium concluded with a lively question and answer period.

In the paper session that followed, Dr. George Howe, Chairman of the Science Department of Los Angeles Baptist College, presented an excellent paper on "Homology, Analogy, and Innovative Teaching," before an audience of several hundred. Howe pointed out that the concept of homology (possession by man and animals of similar structures and functions) was conceived originally by scientists who were creationists, and was accepted by them as evidence that God, the Master Planner, had used a master plan in creation, modifying an overall plan to meet the particular needs of each organism. He suggested a number of experiments that students could perform that would demonstrate the plausibility of the creation model.

Dr. Gish concluded the creationists' portion of the program by presenting a paper on "Speculations and Laboratory Experiments Related to Theories on the Origin of Life." He pointed out the fallacies and weaknesses in such work and claimed that the origin of life by evolutionary processes would not only have been highly improbable, but would actually have been impossible.

The convention ended Saturday morning with a symposium on "Evolution and the Courts." Instead of this vital panel including both creationists and evolutionists, it was loaded with ardent evolutionists. These included two of the officials of the NABT governing board who had brought pressure to bear on the program committee of the 1971 convention to cancel the panel on this same subject scheduled for the 1971 convention. They forced cancellation of this panel because it was to include two creationists, Moore and Gish, in addition to two evolutionists. These were the officials who also, no doubt, were responsible for the instructions to Dr. Cory to present a rebuttal to the Creationists, mentioned earlier.

These panel members, after wasting much time talking about the Scopes Trial, claimed that the issue here in

California, where the State Board of Education had issued a mandate in 1969 that evolution must be taught only as a theory and that creation must also be taught, was the issue of fundamentalist religion on one hand versus science on the other. They insisted that academic freedom would be violated if teachers were instructed to present both views rather than only evolution theory!

During the discussion period that followed, Dr. Gish pointed out that the real issue was not that of fundamentalist religion versus science, but of science versus science, or the right of teachers and students to consider competing theories concerning origins. He pointed out that those groups which had worked so diligently to eliminate the anti-evolutionist laws, which were unconstitutional, now were insisting that only one position, the evolutionary view, be taught, which is equally unconstitutional.

Since the panel members had attempted to appear self-righteous in their ostensible plea for academic freedom, Dr. Gish pointed out that these men had been guilty of unethical conduct and of an abridgement of academic freedom by forcing the cancellation of the 1971 panel and instructing the chairman of the creationist symposium to use time that did not belong to him to present a rebuttal to the creationists. Dr. Gish voiced a plea for real academic freedom and good science — full and free inquiry into both views on origins. Much applause followed Dr. Gish's statement, indicating that many of the biology teachers agreed with his views.

The biology teachers who attended this convention almost to a man have been brainwashed on evolution. Most are unsaved. For the first time they had an opportunity to hear a well-documented, carefully prepared case for creation. Unless absolutely blind, or dulled by prejudice, they must now be aware that there is a credible case for creation. Through the means of this convention, the case for creation has now reached into many hundreds of biology classrooms throughout the United States. This was certainly not the intent of the officials of the National

27

Association of Biology Teachers when they selected the theme of the 1972 convention — "Biology and Evolution"!

MORE UNIVERSITIES HEAR CREATION EVIDENCE

Opportunities for ICR scientists to present the evidence supporting Biblical creationism continue to grow, as both Christian and secular campuses are showing more concern over this issue than at any previous time in the present generation.

Of special interest was the "debate" held on October 11 at the University of Missouri, Kansas City, between Dr. Robert Gentile, well-known Professor of Geology at that institution, and Dr. Henry Morris, Director of ICR, on the creation-evolution question. Over 350 students and faculty members attended. The evolutionist chose to ignore all of Dr. Morris' arguments, which centered especially on the evidence against evolution from the laws of thermodynamics, along with the mathematical absurdities of neo-Darwinian theory and abiogenesis. Instead, Dr. Gentile concentrated on criticizing the "astral visitor" theory of catastrophism (which Dr. Morris pointed out was irrelevant to the discussion, since very few creationists hold this view anyway) and advocating a 19th century uniformitarian approach to sedimentation theory (which Dr. Morris showed by citation from current geological literature is no longer held by even many modern evolutionary geologists). Dr. Gentile also ignored the evidence of the systematic gaps in the fossil record, but did finally recognize that the very existence of vertebrate fossils requires catastrophic processes. There has been much interest on the campus since, and the student newspaper itself reported that creationism clearly won the debate. A similar debate has recently been held at the University of California, San Diego. Again a creationist, Dr. Gish, presented strong arguments which his evolutionist opponent, a member of the biology faculty at U.C.S.D., could not answer.

The Institute and its supporters believe that these contacts with college students and teachers around the country will prove to be of vital importance in the re-establishment of sound Biblical and creationists convictions in our nation.

DIRECTOR'S COLUMN

Henry M. Morris, Ph.D.

Many people around the country have the impression that the state of California has passed a law requiring the teaching of creation in its schools and that it has officially adopted creationist textbooks for use in its classrooms.

Unfortunately, neither of these beliefs is based on fact. There is neither a law nor such a textbook adoption as yet, nor have there been any court decisions requiring equal treatment of creationism and evolutionism.

In 1969 the California Board of Education, whose members are appointed by the Governor, did issue a directive to the effect that creation and evolution should both be taught in the schools, and the sense of this directive was incorporated, over the protests of the science curriculum commission appointed by the Board, into the official Science Framework of the state's school system.

However, nothing has yet been done to implement this directive. The textbook publishers have been unwilling to make any changes in their textbooks, and the various scientific and educational organizations have been vigorously opposing it. Even the most prestigious of all scientific establishments, the quasi-governmental National Academy of Science, has departed from its usual academic aloofness to lobby in California against creationism!

In the meantime, various citizens around the country have either instituted or are contemplating lawsuits to try to *force* the teaching of creation along with evolution in the public schools. Others are trying to sponsor legislation to this same effect.

Frankly, I believe that such politico-legal actions, however well-intentioned, are ill-advised and may do more harm than good to the creationist movement. Even if favorable laws or court decisions are obtained (neither of which is likely in the modern judicial and political climate), this would not insure that creation would actually be taught. Implementation would, in fact, be almost impossible under present conditions. Teachers do not know how to teach scientific creationism, even if they were willing to do so, and there are almost no textbooks or other materials yet available to help them to do so.

Furthermore, the reaction of the press to such a political or judicial imposition of creationism would be devastating.

A new "creation law" or court decision, especially at the federal level, would unleash a barrage of journalistic bombast and ridicule that could well destroy all the gains achieved by creation scientists in recent years.

For these reasons, we recommend that creationists *not* adopt the political route as the means to their ends. The slower route — that of strategic research, high-quality textbook preparation, and educational programs in schools, scientific organizations, churches, etc. — is the only way that offers real promise of lasting results.

However, if movements *do* develop in certain places for legislation or judicial action, we strongly urge that promoters of these actions stress the *scientific*, rather than the religious, aspects of the issue. Testimony from qualified creationist scientists stressing that creation is a better *scientific* model of origins than evolution is essential. Attempts to force teaching of the *religious* doctrine of creation in the public schools are unrealistic at best. In view of all we stand to lose by the hysteria that the latter would cause, a legal action based mainly on the religious issue should be avoided. In fact, I believe that *any* kind of legal action in this connection should be postponed at least until we have a far better stock of creationist textbooks than we now have and until we have achieved a considerably higher level of respect and recognition in the academic communities. This must be our immediate goal.

In the meantime, we want to wish all readers of *Acts & Facts* a wonderful time of blessing during the Christmas season and the year ahead. We rejoice again as we remember that our great Creator loved us enough to become our Saviour. As we rejoice in His first coming, let us remember also that as "Christ was once offered to bear the sins of many . . . unto them that look for Him shall He appear the second time without sin unto salvation" (Hebrews 9:28).

CALIFORNIA SCHOOL DECISION
VICTORY OR DEFEAT?

Most of our readers are aware of the public hearing held by the California State Board of Education on November 9 concerning the inclusion of scientific creation in science texts used in California public schools. Of the 22 scientists that offered testimony, eleven were creationists. Dr. George Howe and Dr. Duane Gish, members of the Creation Research Society, were among those who testified. Portions of their testimony were broadcast nationwide on ABC-TV newscasts. The meeting generated world-wide attention, setting the stage for the December Board meeting when the issue was to be decided and science books adopted.

At the December meeting, the Board adopted the science books recommended by the Curriculum Development Commission. The Commission is a citizens group appointed by the Board to examine and recommend textbooks for adoption. Presently dominated by evolutionists, the Commission membership, however, does include some creationists, one of those being Mr. Vernon Grose, the Commission's primary spokesman for creationism.

Though none of the books recommended by the Curriculum Commission included creation, the Board approved their adoption, subject to revision as directed by the Board.

Due to considerable pressure brought upon the Commission by creationists on the Commission, the Board, and by those in public testimony, the Curriculum Commission unanimously recommended to the Board:

"That on the subject of discussing origins in the science textbooks, the following editing be done prior to execution of a contract (with a publisher):

1. That dogmatism be changed to conditional statements where speculation is offered as explanation for origins.
2. That science discuss "how" and not "ultimate cause" for origins.

3. That questions yet unresolved in science be presented to the science student to stimulate interest and inquiry processes."

Within the Board, little disagreement existed concerning the first two Commission recommendations; however, evolution advocates questioned the intent of the third recommendation. After long debate, Mr. Eugene Ragle, a Board member and strong creationist, offered the following resolution in order to clarify the issue:

"That the unanimous recommendation of the Curriculum Commission presented November 9th be approved and adopted by this Board with the editing to be subject to review by this Board and such editing to make provision for both Evolutionism and Creationism theories."

The resolution received five votes in favor and three against. Six votes are required for Board action; consequently, the resolution failed. The Board then unanimously adopted the first two recommendations of the Curriculum Commission. A committee was appointed to edit the books. The committee includes Dr. John R. Ford, a strong creationist and member of the Board; Dr. David Hubbard, President of Fuller Theological Seminary and a member of the Board who had supported the resolution to include creation; Dr. Richard Bube, a professor at Stanford and a theistic evolutionist; Dr. Robert Fischer, professor at Dominguez State College and also a theistic evolutionist; and three members of the staff of the Department of Education.

Dr. Ford announced his intention to reintroduce, at the January meeting, the resolution to include creation. Mr. Tony Sierra, a member of the Board and a strong creationist, was unavoidably absent from the December meeting and it was anticipated that his vote at the January meeting would carry the cause for creation.

Between the December and January meetings, however, one of those who had voted for inclusion of creation apparently decided to switch his or her vote. If the resolution to include creation had been introduced, it would have been defeated. Dr. John Ford then decided to abandon, for the present, efforts to include creation in science texts. He offered instead a resolution stating "special creation and all other philosophies related to origins will be included in *social science texts* to be adopted in 1976" (we do not yet have an official copy of his resolution and must rely on a telephone report). The resolution was adopted unanimously by the Board. Evolutionists have temporarily succeeded in keeping scientific creationism out of California science texts. We can consider these results pessimistically as defeat or optimistically as partial victory. Unfortunately, evolution theory will remain as the sole explanation for origins in California science texts; however, a number of advances for scientific creationism were registered: (a) evolution will be taught only as a theory, and all dogmatic statements related to the theory will be removed; (b) creation will eventually be included in California textbooks, but under the heading of philosophy; (c) millions of people have been made aware of the fact that not only Biblical scholars advocate special creation, but also many qualified scientists; (d) action in this state has encouraged citizens of other states to also initiate action in order to secure equal emphasis for creationism in their own schools.

Furthermore, it should be pointed out that a strict interpretation of the Board's resolution stating, "creation and all other philosophies related to origins must be included in social science texts" should also include evolutionism. Evolutionism is just as much a philosophy as is the concept of special creation. Such an interpretation will amost certainly not be made, however.

Some citizens and legislators of California have begun preparation of legislation for introduction in the California legislature requiring inclusion of scientific creation in science texts. Similar legislative action is under way in Wisconsin and Michigan.

We at the Institute believe that the most effective weapon available in this battle, in addition to prayer, is education. Most scientists, teachers, students, and general public are appallingly ignorant of the fallacies and weaknesses in the evolution theory and of the tremendous case for scientific creation. The Institute, through its program of research, writing, radio, publications seminars, and summer institutes, is dedicated to the task of education in Biblical and scientific creation. Let us continue to stand together in prayer and labor in this battle to win hearts and minds for the Lord.

DIRECTOR'S COLUMN
Henry M. Morris, Ph.D.

The first month of a New Year is an excellent time to review the activities of the past year. There have been many problems and pressures, but God's grace has been abundant, and it has been a wonderful year in His service. Some of the highlights have been:

1. The creation mini-symposium at the annual convention of the National Association for Biology Teachers, where Dr. Duane Gish was able to give two strong creationist papers to over 1,000 biology teachers and make a tremendous impression, receiving international news coverage.

2. The decision of the California Board of Education to require revisions in the state's science textbooks. While we certainly don't take credit for this, our contacts with Board members, our continual promotion of scientific creationism around the state, and Dr. Gish's testimony at the November meeting of the Board undoubtedly had a good effect.

3. The Summer Institutes on Scientific Creationism held in San Diego and Springfield, Missouri, each consisting of two credits of graduate-level course work, co-sponsored by Azusa Pacific College, Evangel College, and Christian Heritage College. In addition, one-credit intensive workshops on creationism were held in San Diego, Fresno, and Hume Lake, co-sponsored by Azusa Pacific College, Pacific College, and Christian Heritage College, as well as the National Educators' Fellowship.

4. Publication of Dr. Gish's two books, *Evolution? The Fossils Say NO!* and *Speculations and Experiments Related to the Origin of Life* and of my books, *A Biblical Manual on Science and Creation*, and *The Remarkable Birth of Planet Earth*.
5. The expedition to Mount Ararat, led by John Morris, during this past summer. Although they did not find the Ark (next time, Lord willing!), the trip did produce valuable photographs, significant exploration, important contacts, and much evidence of God's power and leading.
6. Important meetings on 20 secular college and university campuses, where the scientific evidence for creation was favorably received by large numbers of students. In addition, meetings were held at numerous public high schools and with various groups of scientists and teachers. Also, meetings were held at 20 Christian colleges.
7. Inauguration of a weekly radio program, SCIENCE, SCRIPTURE, AND SALVATION.
8. Geographically, meetings were held by either Dr. Gish or myself in 20 different states during the year, in churches, schools, on radio and television, civic clubs, seminars, summer conferences, etc. The number of actual messages totals approximately 400 and the total attendance (not including radio and television), probably around 50,000.

Projects in which we are actively engaged at present, in addition to frequent speaking engagements and trying to keep up with a deluge of correspondence and requests for help on various problems all over the country, include the following:

1. Editing and publishing the world history textbook *Streams of Civilization*, by Albert Hyma.
2. Writing a comprehensive *Handbook on Creation and Modern Science*, now nearly complete.
3. Writing a comprehensive *Handbook of Practical Christian Evidences*, now nearly complete.
4. Editing and publishing several Technical Monographs,

including (a) *Critique of Radiometric Dating*, by H. Slusher; (b) *The Center of the Earth*, by A. Woods; and several others.

5. Expansion of our weekly radio program, SCIENCE, SCRIPTURE AND SALVATION, now heard on over 40 stations each week.

6. Planning week-long, two-credit Summer Institutes to be held this summer in San Diego, California; Springfield, Missouri, Lynchburg, Virginia; Calgary, Alberta, Canada; and probably Seattle, Washington.

7. Continued publication of the monthly newsletter *ICR ACTS & FACTS;* in the future each will contain an insert dealing with an article of permanent interest, and these will also be made available for quantity purchase as the *ICR IMPACT SERIES.*

8. Planning summer expedition to Mount Ararat, Lord willing and providing.

There are many other writing, teaching, and research projects under consideration, but limited time and personnel (which, being interpreted, means limited finances) preclude their active implementation for the time being.

You will also be interested in knowing that Christian Heritage College, of which ICR is a division, has excellent prospects for next year. Enrollment for the present semester totalled 92, and we expect this will at least double next year. Prospects are good for the purchase of a beautiful and complete campus next semester. This semester, Dr. Gish is teaching our regular course in Scientific Creationism and I am teaching courses in Genesis and in Practical Christian Evidences. We will have our first graduating class (probably three students) in June.

Doors of all kinds are opening everywhere, and we believe we are on the threshold of the most important year in the history of the creationist movement. We appreciate greatly your prayers and encouragement. We trust that you also will have a wonderful year in the Lord's service in 1973.

PRESENT THE CREATION MODEL AT UCSD

Editor:

On Thursday, November 16, Dr. Duane Gish, Ph.D. in Biochemistry from U.C. Berkeley, and Associate Director of the Institute for Creation Research in San Diego, presented a small portion of the body of scientific evidence against the Theory of Evolution. His talk centering on, "Creation, Evolution, and the the Fossil Record," compared and contrasted the inherent assumptions of the two models, Creation and Evolution. Throughout the course of his talk, predictions from each model were examined and evaluated in relation to and on the basis of their consistency with the fossil evidence, fossils being our most direct link with the prehistoric past.

The evolutionary model presupposes that present-day life has arisen as a result of naturalistic, gradual changes from the inanimate to the animate with subsequent increases in complexity and diversity. The fossil record should therefore reveal obvious intermediate transitional forms linking the species. On the other hand, the Creation Model assumes the existence of a Creator and a series of direct creative acts. On this basis we should expect to find sudden outbursts of life in the fossil record. Concerning the actual fossil record, to this date no undisputable transitional forms have been found in the strata. It reveals rather, the sudden outbursts of life as predicted by the Creation Model and ignored by the Evolutionary Model. Dr. Gish brought a number of points into consideration, among them a thermodynamic question. Evolution as it occurs in an open system is contrary to the second law of thermodynamics, namely that there is an ever increasing tendency towards randomness — not increasing complexity. Pre-existing living forms (i.e., fertilized egg upwards) possess a "mechanism" in the form of DNA to circumvent this, but only temporarily, they too must eventually succumb to the forces of entropy.

The lecture lasted one hour and a half following which a creative discussion evolved. Participating in the discussion was Dr. Russell Dolittle, Revelle Biochemist, who challenged Dr. Gish to return to the campus for the purpose of presenting, in classroom setting, an in depth comparative study of the two theories.

Recently there has been some controversy concerning whether creation should be given, so to speak, equal time in the state's schools as a logical alternative to the Theory of Evolution. Dr. Gish's presentation was well conceived and reasonably presented. It demonstrated to us if there is another side to the story we as students deserve to hear it. In good conscience we disagree with James D. Watson of Harvard who said that, "Today the Theory of Evolution is an accepted fact for everyone but a fundamentalist minority, whose objections are not based on reasoning but on doctrinaire adherence to religious principles" [*Molecular Bioloby of the Gene*, pg. 2). In the interests of academic freedom, and due to the fact that the creation model has been shown to be scientifically plausible, we recommend its presentation alongside that of the Evolutionary Model here at UCSD.

Tom Cantor
Bill Sjaholm
Biology Majors, Revelle College

OVERFLOW CROWD HEARS OKLAHOMA UNIVERSITY DEBATE

Football was not the only topic of conversation in Norman in January. It is difficult to find evolutionist scientists who are willing to debate creationist scientists, but ICR Technical Advisory Board member Ed Blick was able to arrange such a debate at the University of Oklahoma student union (Dr. Blick is Professor of Aerospace Engineering at Oklahoma).

On the night of the debate, January 15, over 1,000 students attempted to crowd into the 500-seat auditorium. The aisles, the doors, the stage were filled, and at least 200 were turned away.

Debaters for the side of evolution were Dr. David Kitts, Professor of Geology and a former student of the nation's leading evolutionary paleontologist, George Gaylord Simpson, and Dr. Hubert Frings, Professor of Zoology and author of a standard textbook on evolutionary biology. Creationist debaters were Dr. Duane Gish and Dr. Henry Morris of ICR. Each speaker was allotted 20 minutes plus 10 minutes for rebuttal.

No formal vote was taken, but applause and later student reaction seemed clearly to indicate the creationists had presented the stronger case. Though it had been agreed in advance that the discussion would be limited strictly to scientific arguments, with no reference to the Bible or religion, the evolutionists kept bringing up religious arguments, defending evolution as not necessarily precluding religious faith, with their scientific evidence consisting mainly of the small variations and mutations which are observed at the present time.

The two creationists dealt with the two models of origins solely on a scientific basis, showing that the predictions of the creation model always fit the observed facts better than those of the evolution model. Dr. Morris especially stressed the significance of the second law of thermodynamics and Dr. Gish the systematic absence of

40

transitional forms in the fossil records. The two evolutionists were clearly unable to cope with these evidences on a scientific basis. Dr. Kitts, the paleontologist, though admitting that the fossil gaps were a problem to evolutionists, kept insisting on the strange explanation that the gaps were there only because his mentor, Dr. Simpson, had named the fossil fauna to correspond to the gaps! Equally odd was his insistence that the thermodynamic argument against the spontaneous origin of life from non-life was irrelevant since the origin of life was not a part of "evolutionary theory" even though it was a part of evolutionary history!

The ICR representatives also spoke at a special student meeting on the campus at Oklahoma State University to a group of very interested and responsive students. The sponsors had attempted to arrange a similar debate there, but were unable to find any faculty members willing to participate.

The Oklahoma meetings also included a Saturday Creation Seminar, church services on Sunday, and a campus meeting at the Central State University. The Metropolitan Baptist Church of Oklahoma City was host church for the seminar and the university meetings were under the auspices of Campus Crusade.

SPECULATIONS BY A SCIENTIST
RADIOCHRONOLOGICAL CLOCKS IN A SHAMBLES?
Duane T. Gish, Ph.D.

Frederick B. Jueneman, Director of Research, Innovative Concepts Associates, has offered some speculations, which, if true, would reduce all radioactive dating methods to a shambles.

Those of us who maintain that Scripture indicates a relatively recent creation, rather than a creation (or evolution) over hundreds of millions of years, have pointed out that the validity of radioactive dating methods depends upon certain unverifiable assumptions. Scientists can accurately determine the *present* ratios of the isotopes involved in dating methods, but have no empirical scientific method for determining the *original* ratios. Neither do they have any real assurance that these ratios have remained undisturbed to the present day.

A mass of radioactive material, under ordinary circumstances, decays at a constant rate. There is absolutely no way of knowing when any one particular atom will decay, however. The one you have under observation (if it were possible to observe a single atom) may decay in the next instant or it may not decay for a billion years. The only thing predictable is that some will decay and some will not. But why this or that particular atom? No one knows.

Science is built upon the premise that every cause has an effect. Jueneman suggests (Industrial Research, September, 1972, p. 15) that the reason the atoms of a radioactive element decay is that particles are being absorbed, the accumulation of which renders the atom unstable. Although these particles are coming in at a steady rate, their paths and angles of incidence are randomly distributed so that their absorption by various atoms in a radioactive element is random. Thus, the decay of these atoms is random, although at an overall steady rate. He suggests that the particles which are being absorbed by radioactive material are neutrinos, neutral particles with a mass only a small fraction of that for the electron. Under ordinary circumstances, neutrinos are radiated towards the earth at a steady rate, and so the rate of radioactive decay of an element is constant.

What would happen, though, should an enormous quantity of neutrinos suddenly flood throughout space? Novae and super-novae are generators of vast quantities of neutrinos, according to astrophysicists. From the remnant left in our sky, scientists believe that just such a super-explosion took place about 1,500 light years from the earth about 11,000 years ago. That remnant is a pulsar called Vela-X (PSR 0833-45).

Jueneman observes, "Being so close, the anisotropic neutrino flux of the super-explosion must have had the peculiar characteristic of resetting all our atomic clocks. This would knock our carbon-14, potassium-argon, and uranium-lead dating measurements into a cocked hat! The age of prehistoric artifacts, the age of the earth, and that of the universe would be thrown into doubt."

Well, whether this really happened or not and whether radioactive decay is caused by neutrinos or other particles, we do not know. Jueneman's suggestions do serve to emphasize, however, that the knowledge we have of the present ratios of radioactive isotopes and of their decay products tells us nothing about their original ratios, and, therefore, tell us nothing about the age of the rocks or of the earth. The present ratios of radioactive elements and of their decay products, we believe, are dependent on the original created state of the rocks and on geochemical and geophysical changes that have taken place since and, thus, have nothing to do with the age of the rocks.

DIRECTOR'S COLUMN
Henry M. Morris, Ph.D.

Of all the possible titles for a director's column, undoubtedly the most mundane, inane, innocuous, bland title is "The Director's Column." I have tried to devise a better one, an urbane, germane, perspicuous, grand title — but am simply at a loss for words!

I could use a euphonious name, such as "The Director's Conspectus" or "The Boss's Glosses," or perhaps a cleverly scientific name such as "The Geologic Column" (but another columnist has already used this one!) or even "The Outer Space." Maybe I should offer a prize (how about an autographed copy of "Design Methods for Flow in Rough Conduits?") to the reader who sends in the best suggestion.

Of course, labels can be either informative or mis-informative, but contents are the same regardless. One of the most misleading examples of mislabeling is employed by those evolutionists who call themselves "creationists." It is remarkable to hear atheistic evolutionists speak of natural selection as a "creative" process and of those who, like themselves, believe in total evolution as "creationists;" but this is exactly the sort of surrealist semantics that many are using today.

There almost seems to be a deliberate plan in operation to deceive the uncritical public as to the real nature of the creation-evolution issue. In Michigan recently I heard the amazing story of how a legislator there had persuaded his colleagues to delete the term "special creation" from a proposed Michigan law requiring the teaching of both creation and evolution in the public schools on the grounds that, to him, special creation meant what people accomplished in bed! The phrase "Biblical creation" was then substituted, probably with the confidence that any law containing this terminology, even if passed, would soon be thrown out by the courts.

However, more disturbing even than atheistic creationists and political creationists are those religious creationists who claim they believe in *both* creation and evolution. To them, evolution is God's "method" of creation. Evolution is the process, creation the purpose. The creation story in Genesis is given so that we might understand that God is Creator, but it does not intend to tell us *how* He created.

If people wish to believe that God is behind the evolutionary process, it is their privilege, but they should call this belief by its correct name, *theistic evolution* — not creation. They have learned, however, that "creation" is a more acceptable term to their religious friends on Sunday, even though it is better to be known as an evolutionist among their professional colleagues the rest of the week.

So they wish to use creation and evolution as synonymous terms, depending on cultural context. Perhaps they could be called evolutionary creationists — or perhaps creationary evolutionists. One thing is certain, they ought *not* to be called creationists, un-modified.

Further, such a point-of-view, regardless of the label, is

really a contradiction in thought, as well as in terms. Theistic evolution is about as logical as "Christian atheism" or "flaming snowflakes." If evolution is true, then there have been three billion years of suffering and death in the world of living things leading up to man. Billions of animals suffered and died, for no apparent reason. Multitudes even of species have died out. It does seem that, if God used evolution, He used the most wasteful, most cruel process, that He could possibly conceive by which to produce man. But the God of the Bible is not that kind of God!

If they want to believe in evolution, ok. It's a free country. But they should not blame God for it. He would never do it that way!

When real creationists, including those here at I.C.R., speak of creation, they do *not* mean creation by some kind of presently-observable or previously-postulated process. They mean creation by processes of special creative omnipotent command, processes which have never been operative (except in the rare instances of divine miraculous intervention) since the end of the creation period. Creation is *not* evolution. Evolution is *not* creation. The two terms are antonyms, not synonyms.

Christian Heritage College and the Institute for Creation Research will be moving shortly to spacious new facilities on a beautiful campus in the city of El Cajon, a San Diego suburban community. The complete 30-acre campus has been purchased from a former Roman Catholic College by the Scott Memorial Baptist Church of San Diego, the strongly-creationist and evangelistic independent church that has made its facilities freely available to the College and the Institute since their founding three years ago.

In addition to meeting the need for greater office and service space, the new campus contains several large

45

classroom buildings, a spacious library, modern dormitories with accommodations for 300 students, a dining hall, a beautiful 500-seat chapel, and many other needed facilities, all within the beautifully-landscaped foothill campus. Athletic facilities include a soccer field, tennis-basketball courts, and an Olympic-size outdoor swimming pool.

College classes and Institute activities are scheduled to move to the new campus in April. The I.C.R. San Diego Summer Institute on Scientific Creationism will be conducted in the new facilities July 9-13.

Mail will continue to be received at the present address, 2716 Madison Avenue, San Diego, California 92116. Prospective students or others who are interested in the program of the College are invited to write for a copy of the new illustrated catalog.

REPRINT

BOARD UPHOLDS 'CREATION'
BAN FOR TEXTBOOKS

SACRAMENTO — The state Board of Education yesterday came within one vote of reversing its decision last month to keep any mention of the creation out of science textbooks.

They voted 5-2 in favor of a motion to include some mention of alternative theories on the beginning of life to counterbalance that of evolution now in school texts.

A sixth vote would have passed the motion. Three of the 10 board members were absent and two of those have voted against the issue in the past. The other is a new member.

Heads Seminary

In voting against the issue, Board Chairman Newton L. Steward was joined by Dr. David A. Hubbard, who heads a theological seminary in Pasadena.

The motion to include creation came from San Diego member Dr. John R. Ford. The other San Diego member, Tony N. Sierra, said he could not understand how anyone could support religion and attack science and then vote against including the creation in science textbooks.

Hubbard said he was not "voting against God," he still believed in "God the Father, Maker of Heaven and Earth," but he did not think the board could come up with any wording to put in science textbooks that would satisfy the public or the board.

Warns Board

He also said that if the board did not make a decision quickly, there would be no science books in the schools at all.

REPRINT

OKLAHOMA DAILY
Thursday, January 18, 1973
Norman, Oklahoma

To the editor:

The debate between the exponents of evolution, Dr. David B. Kitts, geology, and Dr. Hubert Frings, Zoology, and the exponents of creation, visiting Drs. Duane Gish and Henry Morris, last night in Meacham auditorium calls for comment, and here's mine.

Right or wrong I had the distinct impression that the exponents of creation made a point and the exponents of evolution tried to avoid the point.

The point was that there are missing fossil records of the change or transition from one form of life to another, i.e., fish to mammal, reptile to bird, which makes the evolutionist theory of one continuous development of life untenable because it cannot be scientifically proved, i.e., supported by processes or causes which are observable, or rationally deduced.

The point was avoided by careful word manipulation that centered upon which do you start with — the theory or the evidence? If the accompanying verbiage confused or distracted no one else from the main point, it did me!

There were heartening words that came out of the debate which softened my fundamentalist hide toward the evolutionist.

Take the statement from one of the evolutionists that some (many or few, he didn't say) evolutionists believe in God. That is good news, unless these evolutionists believe in God like some Christians believe in Christ.

Robert Foster
OU Graduate

Greater Ararat. 17,000 ft. elevation is the historic resting place of Noah's Ark.

UNIVERSITY DEBATE
DEBATE AT SACRAMENTO STATE COLLEGE

On March 1 in the Music Auditorium of Sacramento State College, Sacramento, California, a debate was held between world-famous evolutionist Dr. G. Ledyard Stebbins, Chairman of the Department of Genetics, University of California, Davis, his evolutionist colleague; Dr. Richard M. Lemmon, Associate Director, Chemical Biodynamics Laboratory, University of California, Berkeley; and Dr. Duane Gish, Associate Director of the Institute for Creation Research, and his fellow creationist, James C. Boswell, who earned a B.S. degree in chemical engineering and an M.A. degree in business from Texas A. and I. University and who is presently the pastor of Christian Disciples Church, Carmichael, California. Pastor Boswell had arranged the debate. Dr. Wesley Jackson of Sacramento State was in charge of details.

A week or so before the debate it became obvious that the 450-seat Music Auditorium would be woefully inadequate to accommodate the crowd. Rev. Boswell repeatedly requested that the debate be switched to a larger auditorium, but Dr. Jackson refused. As expected, a crowd of from 1,000 to 1,500 people or more came to witness the debate. Many more people were turned away than could be admitted to the auditorium.

The format of the debate was to have Lemmon, Gish, Stebbins, and Boswell, each speak for 20 minutes, to be followed by 5 minute rebuttals. Dr. Lemmon, after noting that Gish and Boswell were both members of the Creation Research Society whose members accept a literal interpretation of the Bible, spent most of his time ridiculing the Bible and demeaning scientists who were not evolutionists. He actually wasted 20 minutes of the evolutionists' time, since he never once discussed any scientific evidence related to the question being debated: "which model offers the best explanation for origins, special creation or organic evolution?"

49

Dr. Lemmon's specialty is chemical research related to evolutionary theories on the origin of life. Yet, not once during the entire evening did Lemmon refer to his work, or to any other such work, in support of evolution. It seems incredible that a man who is devoting his life to research on certain aspects of evolution theory would fail to mention the results of that research in support of this theory. Perhaps Dr. Lemmon feels that this work offers no real support for the evolution theory.

Lemmon implied that scientists who are creationists are not real scientists (he used the words, "We scientists," in referring to evolutionists). In his rebuttal, Gish pointed out that not only had Lemmon failed to mention any aspect of his own research in support of evolution but that such prominent evolutionists as Drs. J.D. Bernal and Peter T. Mora had explicitly stated that the origin of life was outside the scientific domain (see Gish's ICR Monograph #1, *Speculations and Laboratory Experiments Related to Theories on the Origin of Life*). Thus, while Lemmon was accusing creationist scientists of being non-scientists, he was devoting his own career to research that even evolutionists admitted was not science!

In his formal presentation, Gish made three main points in the brief time available. He pointed out that since the scientific method always involves intelligence, design, and purpose, creation, which required intelligence, design, and purpose, is a more truly scientific explanation for origins than the hypothetical evolutionary process, which is totally devoid of intelligence, design, and purpose.

Gish then pointed out that Stebbins, speaking as Stebbins, the scientist, had said in 1967 that "Organized structure, specific function, heredity, development, and evolution are the distinctive properties of life which are not even approached by those of the inanimate physico-chemical universe." Gish then related that Stebbins, speaking as Stebbins, the evolutionist, had said in 1972 (after citing evidence allegedly supporting a possible abiogenic origin of certain molecules found in living things): "The arrangement of these molecules into

50

functional systems that were self-reproducing, and their evolution finally into the first cellular organisms, can be explained by processes of chemical mutation, recombination, and natural selection similar to processes that have been experimentally demonstrated to be responsible for change of micro-evolutionary order in contemporary organisms."

Gish pointed out the total contradiction between these two statements. Stebbin's first statement emphasizes (correctly) that there is no such thing as heredity, development, and evolution in the inanimate, physico-chemical world, but then his second statement invokes all of these processes in the inanimate, physico-chemical world to explain the origin of life. Hardly anything could be more contradictory! Furthermore, other prominent evolutionists have emphasized that natural selection could not operate before life existed. As a matter of fact, there is no such thing as "chemical mutation, recombination, and natural selection" at the physico-chemical level except in the minds of evolutionists.

Gish then cited statements of the premier evolutionary paleontologist, Dr. George Gaylord Simpson, and of the well-known evolutionist, Dr. Richard B. Goldschmidt, that document the fact that gaps in the fossil record between higher categories of plants and animals (which creationists believe constitute the created kinds of Genesis) are regular and systematic. Gish pointed out that this remarkable absence of the transitional forms predicted by evolution theory is fatal to the theory but exactly as predicated on the basis of special creation.

Dr. Stebbins, in his formal presentation, showed a slide of the skeletal structure of Archaeopteryx, allegedly the oldest known bird, and the skeletal structures of two reptiles. Stebbins claimed that one of the reptiles looked more like Archaeopteryx than the other and that this was evidence for the evolutionary origin of birds from reptiles. The most obvious thing his slide illustrated to many in the audience is the tremendous gap between reptiles and birds not bridged by transitional forms. Gish, in his rebuttal, merely quoted the statement by W.E. Swinton, an evolutionist and authority on birds, that "The origin of birds is largely a matter of deduction. There is no fossil evidence of the stages through which the remarkable change from reptile to bird was achieved."

Most of the remainder of Stebbins' presentation was evidence he adduced from the fossil record of plants he believed supported evolution theory. Gish had already quoted in his presentation a statement by the prominent Cambridge University botanist and evolutionist, E.J.H. Corner, that the fossil record of plants is in favor of special creation. Dr. Stebbins is to be commended for his part in the debate. His was a reasoned approach. He confined his discussion to the subject in question and presented in logical order the evidence he felt supports the theory of evolution.

Boswell, in his presentation, showed that there is a clear contradiction between the Second Law of Thermodynamics and the theory of evolution. He illustrated this fact by pointing out that the construction of the auditorium in which the audience was seated required intelligence, design, and purpose coupled with specific energy transformations utilizing humans and inanimate machines. This is creation. If the same building is merely allowed to stand for several hundred years, however, being acted on by random applications of energy and natural processes such as sun, wind, rain, and oxidation, it will crumble to dust. Natural processes always tend to proceed from complex to simple, from an organized state to a disorganized state. Evolution theory postulates that just the opposite occurred and that particles gave rise to people.

Boswell described in brief detail the incredible complexity of a living cell and challenged the evolutionists to explain how all of this could have arisen from chaos by natural processes. There is no answer, of course, to this question.

Gish, during the general discussion that followed, pointed out that Leclerq had published the fact that spores and fragments of woody plants, including those of pine trees, had been found in Cambrian rocks. He also quoted Daniel Axelrod of the University of California, Davis, as reporting the finding of spores of 60 genera of woody plants in Cambrian strata. Stebbins was dumbfounded by these statements (evolutionists have long claimed that woody plants, such as the conifers, did not arise until over 200 million years after the Cambrian, and that, in fact, no land animals or plants of any kind existed at the time of the Cambrian). He challenged Gish to produce the references. Gish reached down into his voluminous file (carefully categorized) to produce the references and quotations. Stebbins, shocked and disturbed, said that he was going to talk to Professor Axelrod about this matter as soon as he returned to Davis. It is amazing that Stebbins was completely unaware of these facts, so vitally important to evolution theory and paleobotany, his chosen specialties.

Both Rev. Boswell and Dr. Gish found opportunities before the close of the evening to give their Christian testimonies. Much applause followed each testimony.

The entire debate was televised by Sacramento State College, and portions were televised by a local TV station and portions of their recordings were used on their newscasts the following day.

Apparently this debate marks the end of encounters between Dr. Stebbins and members of the Institute. Recently, it has been reported to us that in reply to a request that followed the Sacramento debate, Dr. Stebbins stated that he would refuse to debate Dr. Gish, Dr. Morris, or anyone else from the Institute for Creation Research.

DIRECTOR'S COLUMN
Henry M. Morris, Ph.D.

The popularity of our *I.C.R.* newsletter *ACTS &
FACTS* has exceeded our expectations. Each issue sees
several hundred new names added to the mailing list, all
by request, and the reactions from readers have been
uniformly favorable and even enthusiastic. One of the
most popular features has been the reporting of public
debates, scientific meetings, and other similar occasions at
which creationist scientists have been able to present
strong evidence for creation to secular audiences. Most
Christians have been reluctant, ever since the days of the
Scopes trial, to challenge evolutionists on their own
grounds, and it has been a great encouragement to many
to learn that a thorough-going creationist system is
begining to make a real impact in the scientific and
educational worlds.

Our own *I.C.R.* staff members are not the only
scientists now receiving frequent opportunities of this
sort. The outstanding science faculty at Bob Jones
University, under the chairmanship of Dr. Joe Henson
(who is also a member of the I.C.R. Technical Advisory
Board), has been on numerous secular campuses and, at
this writing, is preparing for a scheduled debate soon with
evolutionist faculty members at Notre Dame University.
Dr. John Moore, Dr. George Howe, Dr. Ed Blick, Dr.
Tom Barnes, Dr. Walter Lammerts, Dr. Earl Hallonquist,
and many other creationist scientists are now in great
demand for lectures and discussions of this type.

In general, creationists have been able to present a
strong case in such meetings. The scientific *facts* are on
our side, even though we certainly don't yet have answers
to *all* the problems.

At the same time, we must certainly avoid becoming
smug and over-confident. The doctrinaire evolutionists
are becoming alarmed and we can be sure the opposition
will soon begin to increase in intensity. Until now, most of
the leading evolutionists have not taken us seriously, and
they have often come poorly prepared to such

confrontations. In any case, although these meetings are conducted on a scientific level, the battle is really a spiritual battle, and we urge all our Christian readers to make it a matter of regular prayer. "If God be for us, who can be against us" (Romans 8:31).

Those readers who remember the first few issues of *ACTS & FACTS* are aware that, not only has the mailing list greatly increased in size, but also the size of the publication has been greatly enlarged. Obviously the cost of sending it out has, therefore, increased even more. We consider its distribution a missionary ministry, of course, and are more than glad to send it free to all who want it.

Realistically, however, we do hope that most readers will be led to send contributions to *I.C.R.* from time to time, since not only the *ACTS & FACTS* but also all our other activities depend entirely on such contributions. A large number of those on our mailing list are high school and college students, who need and want these materials, but who are unable to help much financially. We have no governmental or denominational backing, of course, so that the work depends on gifts from concerned local churches and individuals, as the Lord leads and enables them to help, as well as on their prayers.

CHRISTIAN TEACHERS' CONVENTION

Dr. Henry Morris was the featured speaker recently at the annual business session of the Christian Educators' Association of the Southeast, meeting in Tampa, Florida, on February 23. This is believed to be the largest gathering of teachers of Christian schools in the world, and almost 3,000 were in the audience to hear Dr. Morris speak on "Teaching Creation Without Compromise."

CREATION HITS CAMPUS NEWSPAPERS

Recently advertisements like those pictured below began appearing in college newspapers in Southern California.

The College Ad Project (CAP) was conceived by Robert Seelye, an insurance executive from La Mirada, California, who had a strong desire to reach the college student on the secular campus with the fact that special creation was a more viable and logical explanation of how we got here than the molecules-to-man theory of evolution. He also wanted them to know that evolution was not the only explanation of origins and that many qualified scientists believe special creation offers a much more realistic explanation and, therefore, a more "scientific model" for life's beginnings.

In short, "get the college student to realize there is another side to the evolution question and start thinking for himself."

The molecules-to-man theory has dominated the public school system so totally that the majority of college students aren't aware of an alternative in special creation that fits the facts of science much better.

During the first few weeks of this pilot program in three campus newspapers, approximately 200 students and professors have written for more information about special creation. Within a few days they had received a packet of information from the Institute with special articles and educational material. After receiving the first packet, if he wants to know more about the Creator/Designer of the Universe, the student may write for another packet designed to show how the Creator relates to him personally.

The following excerpts from letters give an indication of the value of this approach to the college student.

"Please send free packet of literature outlining the credibility of special creation. I am anxious to obtain facts on creation and evolution. The past six years, I have been

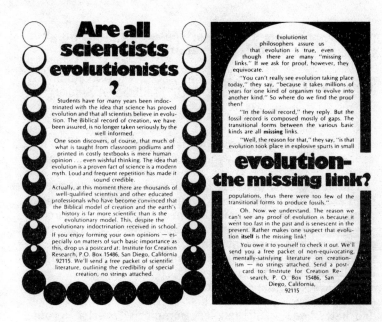
an agnostic, and just recently have decided to do some basic research on the subject." J.W. Cal Poly

"I'm an independent thinker, and very curious (but skeptical), so would you please send me a free eye-opening packet of factual creationist information?" R.Y., N. Hollywood

"I am interested in researching the scientific evidence for creation and making my own mind up as to its authenticity." D.R., Cal Poly

"Please send me the free packet of scientific evidence outlining the credibility of special creation. I haven't made my mind up and want to hear both sides." F.M., Harvey Mudd College

The CAP program is financed entirely with specially designated funds. A CAP account has been set up at ICR into which funds are placed. Advertisements are placed in the campus newspapers with the bills sent to the Institute. The cost of the packet sent out averages 40¢ for postage and materials. By sponsoring the program through ICR, all funds given are tax-deductible.

The opportunity is available to sponsor the CAP program in your area. Additional details are available by writing ICR-CAP Program 2716 Madison Avenue, San Diego, California 92116.

DIRECTOR'S COLUMN
Henry M. Morris, Ph.D.

The new *I.C.R.* book, *Adventure on Ararat*, describing the 1972 I.C.R. expedition to Mount Ararat, has just been published, and I trust you have ordered a copy by now. If not, you are missing one of the most fascinating and exciting stories in recent years. Many people have told us they could not lay the book down, once they had started it, without finishing it.

We are planning, Lord willing, to send another expedition back to Ararat this summer, somewhat larger and better equipped than last summer's "tourist" group. We have applied for permits and trust that, in answer to your prayers, they will be forthcoming.

The financing, of course, is a serious problem. We have adopted the policy that no part of our general funds will be used for this special project, since our regular teaching and writing ministries must be maintained and our income is not sufficient even for these. Accordingly, only gifts designated specifically for the Ararat project are used for this purpose, and each member of the expedition team is responsible for raising his share of the cost.

We believe many of you, like we, are vitally interested in this project and will be praying for its success. Also, there are two ways you can help financially. One, of course, is to make a designated contribution for the Ararat research fund. Please, however, make this in addition to your regular gifts to the I.C.R., as the regular ministries are in critical need of more, not less, support.

Secondly, you can arrange for your church or other

group to invite one of the team members to speak and show slides on Ararat and then take up an offering for the project. It would be necessary, of course, to also provide his travel expenses. Such meetings must be scheduled right away, since the team plans to leave for Turkey early in July. Write or call John Morris here at the I.C.R. office in San Diego to arrange a time for the team member nearest you to speak.

We do not know, of course, what the outcome of the project will be. This, however, is true of any research project; but this could well be the most significant research study of the century, even though the physical and spiritual obstacles are almost overwhelming. We are convinced the Ark is *there* and God is going to unveil and demonstrate it in His time — not before. But when His time *does* come, it is important that someone be there to see the unveiling and document the demonstration!

READERS' COMMENTS

"For all previous data, and this Acts and Facts Packet: thanksgiving and praise be to the Lord."

C.D.S., California

"I believe you're doing one of the most difficult and important tasks of the Church — it is actually long overdue. God bless you."   J.O.L., Ohio

"I attended your meetings last year when you were here. I also purchased your book, A BIBLICAL MANUAL ON SCIENCE AND CREATION. It is fantastic!"

BBC Student, Mo.

THE UNANSWERED CHALLENGE

Evolutionists commonly claim that evolution is a scientific fact and creation a mere religious dogma. This argument is endlessly repeated as the reason why creation should not be taught in the public schools. When challenged to engage in public debate on the relative *scientific* merits of creation and evolution with scientists who are creationists, however, most leading evolutionists exhibit a strange reluctance to defend these claims.

Dr. William V. Mayer is one of the nation's top evolutionary scientists and Head of the Biological Sciences Curriculum Study Center at the University of Colorado, the organization that produced the famous B.S.C.S. high school biology textbooks. These books are saturated with evolutionary philosophy and have been extensively used in the public schools of our country for the past decade. It was largely in reaction to these volumes that the Creation Research Society developed its fine creationist-oriented textbook, BIOLOGY: A SEARCH FOR ORDER IN COMPLEXITY.

Because of the recent upsurge of interest in creationism, Dr. Mayer decided, in his monthly publication, the BSCS NEWSLETTER, to devote an entire issue (November, 1972) to a broadside against the creationists, especially against the Creation Research Society. The articles at best presented only a caricature of creationism.

As president of the Creation Research Society, Dr. Henry Morris, who is also Director of the Institute for Creation Research, decided it was unfair to let this go unchallenged and so wrote Dr. Mayer with a proposal for a public debate on the subject. This letter precipitated an interesting exchange of correspondence, totalling five letters from Dr. Mayer and five from Dr. Morris. Knowing that the readers of ACTS AND FACTS are very interested in this type of dialogue, excerpts from several of Dr. Morris' letters are reproduced below. The last of Dr. Mayer's letters (the only one he gave permission to reprint) is also included.

Although the proposed debate never took place, this correspondence in itself is significant. The letters follow:

January 1, 1973
Dear Dr. Mayer:

As President of the Creation Research Society, I have read with great interest and concern the November, 1972, issue of your BSCS Newsletter. Many creationist scientists feel that you and other writers in this issue of the Newsletter have seriously misunderstood and misrepresented our position in the current creation-evolution controversy.

In order to clarify the issue, especially in the minds of the general public, I would like to propose a public debate on the issue between you and myself, as perhaps two of the leading spokesmen on the two sides. If you prefer a four-man debate, I would propose that the second creationst be Dr. Duane Gish, whom you probably remember from the NABT Convention in San Francisco. Dr. Gish is Associate Director of the Institute for Creation Research and a member of the Board of Directors of the Creation Research Society. The second evolutionist could be anyone of your choosing.

I would propose, furthermore, that the debate be strictly limited to *scientific* aspects of the question. We would not discuss the religious aspects, nor refer in any way to the book of Genesis or to other religious literature. The proposition to be debated could be the following:

"RESOLVED that the special creation model of the history of the earth and its inhabitants is more effective in the correlation and prediction of scientific data than is the evolution model."

I (or we) would take the affirmative and you could take the negative. Or, if you prefer, we can interchange "special creation" and "evolution" and you can take the affirmative.

We would also invite the newspapers and telecasters, in order to publicize the debate. You should urge the students and faculty at the University of Colorado to attend, and we can urge interested creationists in the area to attend, as well as the general public.

I would suggest that the debate be held in Denver, probably at the Civic Auditorium. A nominal admission fee could be charged in order to cover expenses (the creationist movement is *not* well-financed, as your Newsletter suggested!). We would expect no honoraria, of course. If anything is left over after expenses, it can be divided equally between the Creation Research Society and your NABT Fund for legal action against the creationists.

Since you have insisted that evolution is scientific and creationism is not scientific, I hope you will be willing to defend this position in this manner. We would attempt to show, on the other hand, that creationism *can* be discussed objectively and scientifically and, therefore, does deserve recognition as a legitimate scientific model in scientific curricula. Many creationist scientists are convinced that the privileged position of evolutionism in the schools is maintained not by scientific evidence, but by authoritarian proscription. Such a debate hopefully would prove salutary in resolving such misunderstandings on both sides.

Thanks very much for your consideration of this proposal.

Respectfully yours,
Henry M. Morris
Director

January 19, 1973
Dear Dr. Mayer:

Thank you for your kind letter of January 10, I appreciate your generous offer to publish, without comment, my letter of January 1 in the next issue of your BSCS Newsletter. You have my permission to do this, of course.

Your definition of evolution ("Organisms change with time") is not complete, since it does not incorporate the dimension of evolution to which creationists object ("The processes of evolutionary change have developed all forms of life, including man from one or a very few common ancestral forms of life").

No scientific creationist questions the reality of the presently-observable biological phenomena of mutation, natural selection, speciation, etc. These are observable processes of change, and they fit quite well within the creation model. It is the extrapolation of these observable changes into the imagined total evolution of the biosphere which we feel is unscientific and unjustified. It is our understanding, derived from reading in the evolutionary literature, that the general model can be stated somewhat as follows:

"The origins and development of all living and non-living systems in the observable universe are attributable to naturalistic, mechanistic processes and properties which are presently in operation and which are, therefore, capable of scientific examination and confirmation."

The creation model, on the other hand, could be stated in some such terms as the following:

"The origin and development of the major categories of living and non-living systems in the observable universe must be explained in terms of a unique period of special creative processes in the past, which are no longer in operation and which, therefore, cannot be examined experimentally in the present."

The creation model does not preclude the origin of new varieties or species, but it does postulate definite limits to such changes. It further implies that any changes which, as it were, attempt to transgress these created boundaries will result in deterioration rather than improvement of the created kinds.

Although it is true that these aspects of the creation model are taught in the Bible, they do not depend on the Bible. The two models lend themselves very directly to

63

the comparative prediction and correlation of data in the natural world. All of this can be discussed completely without reference to the Bible or other religious literature or doctrines.

I hope, therefore, that you will agree to the proposed debate, as suggested in my previous letter.

Sincerely yours,

Henry M. Morris
Director

February 21, 1973
Dear Dr. Mayer:

Yesterday I received two letters from you, both dated February 16, and so hasten to reply before leaving town for several days.

I appreciate your kindness in reproducing my letter of January in the February issue of your BSCS Newsletter. In return, if you will give us permission, we will be happy to reproduce any or all of your three letters in our own newsletter (ACTS & FACTS, published monthly by the Institute for Creation Research).

Since most of the complaints lodged in your two letters of February 16 dealt with either the Bible-Science Association or the Creation-Science Research Center, perhaps I should explain that these two organizations are controlled and operated by laymen, rather than scientists. The C.R.S. (Creation Research Society) and the I.C.R. (Institute for Creation Research) have no affiliation with or control over either the B.S.A. or the C.S.R.C.

The Creation Research Society is a membership organization of scientists who are creationists. Similarly, the Institute for Creation Research is the research division of Christian Heritage College (San Diego) and is also controlled and operated by scientists. The main purpose of both C.R.S and I.C.R. is to study and promote creationism from primarily a scientific point of view.

Whether you are yet aware of this or not, there are today many hundreds, probably thousands, of qualified scientists who have become convinced (in spite of their evolutionist indoctrination in school and college) that evolution is completely inadequate as a scientific theory and that creationism provides a better framework for scientific interpretation.

You expressed concern that creationists do not send out their literature to anyone except those who agree with them. However, I can assure you that we are extremely anxious to get evolutionists to read our literature! Cost is a problem, of course. We have no funds from government, foundations, industry, etc., so continually have to operate very frugally.

Now, getting back to the question of debate. I have tried to assure you, and will do so again, that I (as well as Dr. Gish, if you elect to have a four-man debate) wish to deal with this question strictly on a scientific basis. It really makes no difference whether we use the term "model" or "theory" or whatever you prefer. We normally use "model" (at least those in the Creation Research Society do) because we recognize there is no experimental test that can either demonstrate or falsify creation. By the very concept, creation is not taking place today, and that is the very point at issue.

But exactly the same objection applies to evolution! There is no experimental test that can either confirm or falsify the general "theory" of evolution.

Creationists are as familiar as you are with the phenomena of mutation, speciation, recombination, hybridization, etc., and it is only these processes which the evolutionists mean when they talk about the predictive value of evolution as a theory of biologic change.

All such phenomena, however, are just as easily incorporated within the creationist framework, so it is not legitimate to use them as so-called proofs of evolution. This issue is not over these things at all, but over their extrapolation into total evolution over millions of years. It is precisely this extrapolation which is not subject to scientific test, and therefore this dimension of evolution is not really scientific.

You undoubtedly disagree with the above conclusion, but you should at least recognize that *this is the issue* — not present-day processes of minor variations such as can actually be observed, and which both creationists and evolutionists accept and utilize.

Now, once again, it is *this* dimension of evolution — the total evolution concept, molecules-to-man — that the millions of creationists in this country are concerned about. I should think that, if you *really* believe evolution in this sense is scientific and creation is unscientific, that you would welcome a chance to demonstrate this to a wide audience in a well publicized open debate with the president of the Creation Research Society!

Therefore, I urge you once again to accept this challenge, in the interests of true science and academic freedom.

Respectfully yours,

Henry M. Morris
President

March 15, 1973
Dear Dr. Mayer:

It seems obvious from your three letters, the last dated March 5, that you are not willing to engage in public debate with me or any other qualified creationist scientist on the creation-evolution question. I have repeatedly assured you that I would confine my side of the debate solely to scientific matters, omitting altogether any reference to the Bible or to the religious aspects of the controversy. I have already clearly defined the "creation model" I propose to defend, and the aspects of evolutionism I propose to refute.

If it is true, as you say, that creationist polemics are "based on quotes out of context, misquotes, misinterpretations, and faulty science," I should think you would be happy for this kind of an opportunity to demonstrate it. You apparently feel that I should first submit the complete text of my proposed presentation in the debate to you before you decide whether you are able to debate at all. This is a highly unusual stipulation.

Basically, however, I simply propose to show that the demonstrated *facts* associated with the fossil record, the nature of sedimentary and other geophysical processes, the laws of thermodynamics, and the complexity of living systems, are more easily explained in terms of a fairly-recent special creation of the basic categories of nature and kinds of organisms than in terms of an age-long continuing process of neo-Darwinian evolution.

I might mention that a number of your fellow evolutionists have participated in such debates recently. Just a week ago, Dr. Ledyard Stebbins and Dr. Richard Lemmon debated my colleague, Dr. Gish, and another creationist. Several weeks ago, Dr. Gish and I debated Dr. Frings and Dr. Kitts at the University of Oklahoma. Several other similar debates have taken place. We believe, of course, that in every case the case for creationism was shown to be more scientific than that for evolutionism, though perhaps our opponents thought otherwise! In any case, however, these presentations do permit large and vitally interested audiences to hear both sides and decide for themselves.

Thank you for printing my letter of January 1 in the BSCS NEWSLETTER. I would like again to ask your permission to reprint one or more of your letters in our ICR ACTS & FACTS.

Sincerely yours,

Henry M. Morris
Director

March 29, 1973
Dear Dr. Morris:
    I find it amazing what you find obvious in my letters.

You feel somehow that I am unwilling to debate creationists. In January of this year, I spent two hours over KABC radio in Los Angeles doing exactly that. I've also appeared with creationists on public platforms in San Francisco and will do so this Saturday with John N. Moore in Detroit.

A debate involves argumentation on many sides of a position. In the "debates" in which I have been engaged, the creationists have only one point in mind. Namely, to achieve publicity for their attacks on evolutionary theory. While you accuse me of not being willing to debate, I'm on sounder ground accusing you of not being able to provide me with the creation "model" and the evidence upon which it is based, which I have requested in four letters to you since the first of January. The evidence seems quite clear that there is no creation "model" and no scientific data on which it rests. In a debate, it would be as valuable for me to question the creation "model" as it is for you to question evolutionary theory. However, the way the "debate" ultimately comes to be set up is simply my responding to attacks on evolution. The secretiveness with which you guard the creation "model" allows no discussion of it. Can you see how lively a debate would be if I could ask you for your evidence that the earth is only 4,000 years old? Or why men don't have one less rib than women? Or how you account for the speaking of serpents?

As I have said from the beginning, if you can provide me with detailed information concerning the creation "model" and the evidence upon which it rests, we could have a most interesting debate. Your failure to do so indicates you are not interested in debate at all but rather in a public forum from which to attack the theory of evolution. To this latter, I will not be a part.

Sincerely,

William V. Mayer
Director

P.S. You have asked for permission to print my letters. You may print this one in toto.

April 5, 1973
Dear Dr. Mayer:

You keep asking me to define the creation model, and I have done so repeatedly. I will try once again.

The creation model postulates a period of special creation that was completed in the past, in which the major laws and categories of nature, including the major kinds of plants and animals, were brought into existence by special creative processes which are no longer operative and, therefore, not accessible for quantitative observation. This is in contrast to the evolution model, which assumes that the origin and development of all these systems is to be explained in terms of the same processes that now operate.

In addition, the creation model postulates at least one period of global cataclysmic activity in the past, in which rates of processes were incommensurate with present rates. The evolution model, on the other hand, is premised on uniformitarianism, perhaps allowing local catastrophes but no world-wide cataclysms.

As I understand it, you do not wish to debate on this basis, comparing these two models in terms of their relative ability to predict and correlate observable data. Perhaps you think I should postulate some specific process of creation, but the very nature of the creation model precludes this.

Evolutionists point out, correctly, that creation is non-observable and, therefore, not amenable to the scientific method. But exactly the same thing is true with regard to evolution! The assumption that present processes (mutation, natural selection, etc.) will produce major biologic changes (e.g., on the scale of fish-to-amphibian or ape-to-man) is not subject to empirical test since it requires millions of years. The creationist, of course, includes the phenomena of mutation and natural selection in his own model (as a conservative and deteriorative mechanism, rather than innovative, however) and so processes such as this cannot constitute evidence proving evolution and refuting creation.

Thus, neither evolution nor creation is scientifically testable or demonstrable. That is why we prefer to use the term "model" instead of "theory" for both of them.

As models, they are useful for predicting and correlating data, and we believe the creation model will correlate the greatest amount of scientific data with the minimum amount of secondary explanations to resolve its problems. This is what I had proposed we "debate." I am at a loss to understand why you keep saying I have not told you what the creation model is. I don't know how to say it any more plainly than as above.

The two models can be used to make comparative predictions as to: (1) the character of the array of organisms in the living world; (2) the character of the basic laws of nature; (3) the nature of the fossil record; (4) the nature of biologic change; and many other things. For example, the creation model predicts the basic laws of nature to be conservative and deteriorative, as confirmed by the two laws of thermodynamics, whereas the evolution model has to accommodate the laws by one or more secondary assumptions that are still non-testable.

You force me to assume you are willing to debate this subject only if you can attack Genesis (otherwise why would you bring up such irrelevant subjects as Adam's rib, etc.?, as in your last letter). If you wish to do this, that is all right with me. I *do* believe in the Genesis account of creation and am willing to discuss it if necessary. However, it is not the Genesis narrative which creationists want to see included in the textbooks, but only the basic creation model. Therefore, I proposed that we limit our debate to the two "scientific models," as outlined above.

I do not want "religion" taught in the public schools any more than you do, and this is exactly why we object to the evolutionary philosophy being taught to the exclusion of creationism. Since evolution in the large picture is not testable, it is not science, any more than is creation. People *believe* in evolution, but they don't *see* it, because it moves too slowly. Therefore, it is as much a "religious" theory as is creation, and we object to young people being indoctrinated in the "religion" of evolution without equal exposure to the evidence and arguments supporting creation.

I presume it is too late by now to have a debate on the date originally suggested, but I would still be happy to schedule one at some time in the future, if you would be interested.

Sincerely yours,

Henry M. Morris
Director

Editor's Note: No further communication has been received from Dr. Mayer.

DIRECTOR'S COLUMN
Henry M. Morris, Ph.D.

Dr. Duane Gish and I have just returned from the annual meeting of the Board of Directors of the Creation Research Society in Ann Arbor, Michigan. We have each had the privilege of serving on the Board of the Society ever since it was first founded in 1963. In addition, I have been honored to serve as President of the Society for the past six years.

We have seen the Society grow from an initial committee of ten scientists to its present size of 2,000 members of all types, including approximately 450 voting members (scientists with post-graduate degrees in some natural science). Its Quarterly has become the world's outstanding journal of scientific creationism, and its high school textbook, BIOLOGY: A SEARCH FOR ORDER IN COMPLEXITY, published in 1970, marked a real breakthrough in the field of creationist textbooks.

New officers were elected for the C.R.S. this year, with Dr. Tom Barnes, Professor of Physics at the University of

Texas in El Paso, being elected to serve as President. Of all the creationist scientists in the country, I know of none better prepared to lead the Society at this beginning of its second decade than Dr. Barnes. He is both an outstanding scientist, widely recognized and honored in his field and also a gracious Christian gentleman. He has been a close personal friend of mine for many years and has also been a member of our I.C.R. Technical Advisory Board since its beginning.

The new Vice-President is Dr. Emmett Williams, of the Physical Science faculty at Bob Jones University in Greenville, South Carolina. Dr. Williams is also a long-time friend, having been a faculty colleague of mine in the College of Engineering at Virginia Tech at the time he became a Christian. Elected to the office of Secretary was Dr. Wayne Frair, Chairman of the Science Division at King's College in Briarcliff Manor, New York.

In recent years several other creationist organizations have been formed for specific purposes in this field, including our own Institute for Creation Research. None of these are affiliated in any way with the Society, which is solely a membership organization with the primary purpose of creation research, said research to be published primarily in its Quarterly.

It should also be stressed that I.C.R. likewise has no connection with *any other* creationist organization. Many people have confused I.C.R. with another group, but this impression should definitely be corrected.

Although I.C.R. is not formally affiliated with the Society, we do have similar motivations and purposes and attempt to promote the work of the Society in every way we can. We urge our readers to join the Society, either as voting (scientist) members or as sustaining members. We would be glad to send a membership application form to anyone requesting it.

DIRECTOR'S COLUMN
Duane T. Gish, Ph.D.
Associate Director

In the absence of Dr. Morris, now on an extensive lecture tour of New Zealand, it is my privilege to write the Director's Column this month. Realizing that many of you have just recently become acquainted with our work, I felt perhaps you might be interested in being brought up to date on some of our activities.

Since the founding of the Institute, none of us would have dared to predict what God would accomplish with our very limited personnel and facilities. The case for Biblical and scientific creationism has been presented to many thousands of high school and college students on campuses all over the United States and Canada. The reception accorded our messages by these students has been surprisingly warm, indicating that these young people, in spite of evolutionary propagandists, welcome scientific evidence for a Bible-based faith in God as Lord, Master, and Creator.

These vital messages have reached many thousands of others via seminars, institutes, church services, special meetings, radio, and television. The Master Creator has been presented to believer and unbeliever, to people of all ages and all walks of life.

Three books have been published by the Institute, as well as four technical monographs. All have received wide acceptance and distribution. A history book written with a Christian perspective is now almost ready for the printer, and we have in preparation a comprehensive handbook on science and creation, which we trust will serve as a classic sourcebook on this subject. Other books are under preparation, as well.

We have been operating with a minimum staff in all departments. All staff members have sacrifically given of their time and effort, and others have volunteered their services to accomplish what, at times, seemed to be "the impossible." Hundreds of thousands of pieces of mail have been received and mailed out, and the many other operations of the Institute have been cared for by this limited staff.

An especially heavy speaking and writing load, as well as a deluge of correspondence, has fallen on the scientific staff of the Institute, which has consisted solely of Dr. Morris and myself, except during summer months when we have had the invaluable assistance of Professor Harold Slusher. An examination of our seminar, summer institute, and speakers' schedule will reveal that the scientific staff members only rarely dare to take a day or evening off, and only then with uneasy conscience.

However, rather than complaining, we rejoice that God has given us the opportunity to be part of this vital and unique ministry. Our problem is this: many crucially important projects must be laid aside or delayed because of lack of an adequate staff. The research and writing portion of these tasks can be done only by scientifically trained staff members, therefore only the most urgent projects may be undertaken, and even then, often with considerable delay.

The most urgent need is for textbooks in all fields, written within a Christian and creationist perspective. Only a very limited number of such books are now available, forcing Christian schools to use books written within a humanistic philosophy, all of which are based upon the evolutionary world view, of course.

There are other needs to which we feel we should direct our attention as well: literature of all kinds, directed especially to the Biblical and scientific case for special creation; attractive and informative display material for classroom bulletin boards; a magazine, or magazine-type material, for reaching juniors and teenagers. In addition, an expanded radio ministry, a television series, and films could serve as the means of vastly multiplying the number of those who could be reached.

No doubt highly-competent, scientifically-trained, dedicated Christians could be found to augment our staff and undertake these projects. Our problem is the lack of funds necessary to provide for these additional staff members. We urge God's people to become sufficiently concerned about this cancer of evolution-oriented secular humanism that is destroying the minds and faith of our young people; then the necessary prayer and financial support will be provided to allow for the urgently-needed expansion of our staff.

We trust that you will continue to be partners with us in this great ministry, and that increased interest in this vital work will enable us to move forward for our Lord without hindrance in the days ahead.

COME TO CHRISTIAN HERITAGE

As the fall semester approaches, we would like to give college-age young people and their parents a special invitation to consider Christian Heritage College. With a beautiful new campus near San Diego, Christian Heritage offers an unusual and rewarding educational experience which cannot be duplicated anywhere else.

Consider the following unique aspects of C.H.C.

1. There is no other college, as far as we know, in which all programs include a strong emphasis on Christian evidences and scientific creationism. Each student takes six semester-hours of each of these subjects, as well as a minimum of 18 semester-hours in Bible. Thus he is well prepared to defend and propagate the work of God, regardless of his particular major or future occupation in life.
2. The student has the unique opportunity of close contact with the Institute for Creation Research, with its scientists and varied activities in promoting creationism around the nation. Many of the students, in fact, actually work for the Institute on a part-time basis and all of them maintain a close interest in its work. Again, so far as we know, there is no other college anywhere with this particular type of opportunity.

75

3. Another associated organization (though not directly affiliated with the College) is Family Life Seminars, whose director, Dr. Tim LaHaye is also President of Christian Heritage College. This highly effective, nation-wide ministry is also reflected in Christian Heritage concerns and activities.

4. Christian Heritage College has a number of distinctive degree programs which cannot be found elsewhere. One of these is our new B.S. program in Planetary Science, a uniquely creationist geophysics curriculum. Another is the five-year program in Missionary Aviation, which is a full B.S. program in Missions, plus F.A.A. — designed training in aircraft piloting and maintenance.

In addition to the above unique aspects of Christian Heritage College, other important emphases include: (a) faithfulness to the local church; (b) evangelism and missions; (c) national loyalties; (d) Christian character and conduct; (e) student neatness and modesty; (f) sound doctrinal position, including full inspiration of the Bible, centered in the person and work of Jesus Christ.

Academically, the College has an excellent faculty and places strong emphasis on solid curricular content and high standards of learning. We intend to work diligently to meet all objective standards for regional accreditation as rapidly as possible. B.S. and B.A. programs are now available in 12 different majors, and others are being added as resources permit.

If you are interested in Christian Heritage College, either as a potential student or counsellor of students, or as a prospective supporter of this type of distinctive (and, we believe, badly needed) kind of Christian education, please write us for a free copy of the new C.H.C. Catalog.

BOOKS NEEDED FOR LIBRARY

With its move to the new campus in the San Diego suburb of El Cajon, Christian Heritage College has acquired a fine new library facility. It is hoped that an outstanding library can soon be developed.

Gifts of books to the new library (or of funds designated to purchase books) will be greatly appreciated. Such gifts are tax-deductible. Mrs. Henry Morris, librarian at Christian Heritage College, will be happy to acknowledge gifts of books with a letter itemizing them, which can be used in support of a tax-deduction claim. Books may be shipped, postage collect, to:

LIBRARY, Christian Heritage College
2100 Greenfield Drive
El Cajon, California 92021

All types of college-level books are needed, especially Bible commentaries and reference books, as well as books on missions, Christian biographical studies, and reference works in the natural sciences, history, and education.

THE AGE OF THE SOLAR SYSTEM
(PART I)
Harold S. Slusher, M.S.

Numerous arguments have been concerned with the ages of the earth, the solar system, and the universe as a whole. Though the chronology of geological and astronomical events is based on many dubious assumptions and questionable ventures beyond the province of science, it is absolutely necessary for the evolutionists to try to establish a long chronology.

Most evolutionists believe that life began by a chance process in a shallow sea and that the world we see today came about by gradual and infinitesimal changes, happening by chance and taking place over vast and almost limitless stretches of time. The evolutionist tries to eliminate problems which face his naturalistic scheme of origins by covering the whole issue behind a veil of time.

Thus, long periods of time have become a tenet in the evolutionist's creed. For example, the physical appearance of rocks in the Franklin Mountains, El Paso, Texas, suggests the rapid deposition of sedimentary material and consequent movement of the rocks while in a somewhat unconsolidated or semiplastic state. At one time a geophysicist of the evolutionary faith discussed these rocks and other similar mountain ranges with me and he agreed that the appearance of the rocks suggested that deposition and mountain building happened in rapid succession, but he resisted this conclusion by pleading for a long time through gradual processes for their origin. To him, time solved all the difficulties that the uniformitarian assumptions regarding physical processes seemed to create.

Also, time is fostered as a rationale for the missing links in the evolutionary explanation of the fossils. While discussing the problem of missing links with an evolution-minded geologist, I asserted that the fossil links are still missing and probably were nonexistent. He reminded me that the links might have been present originally and then after subsequent erosion over long time spans, they are not to be found. I remarked that if the links could not be found, one could not know that they were present in the past. At this point, an evolutionist places his faith in slow processes acting over epochs of unknown time to solve this basic difficulty.

There are many fundamental difficulties and limits placed on working into the past. In the second law of thermodynamics, or law of entropy, physicists deal with the natural and continual tendency of the universe toward disorder. It is a study of deteriorative processes. The attempt to work backwards into the past where deteriorative processes have dominated is fraught with many insuperable obstacles. Entropy of the universe is increasing, chaos is gradually replacing order. One cannot measure backward to the beginning by studying the decay processes, as has been shown by authors of past articles in this publication.

One of my college professors once remarked that, even if most or nearly all mutations are harmful to the organism, during a vast period of time a few beneficial mutations would occur and these would produce the upward progress of the organism. He overlooked the effect of lethal mutations upon the organism in the meantime. Given enough time, the evolutionist believes, the improbable becomes probable.

Dr. Harold F. Blum, however points out that an increased time span for a biological system increases the probability of reaction equilibria being set up in the chain and does *not* increase the probability of improbable reaction products being formed.[1] Time cannot supply what the evolutionist needs, even if it existed in the quantities he demands.

Yet, in spite of strong evidence to the contrary of evolution, many people feel that if the earth is very old, evolution will somehow or other be the answer to the question of the origin of the universe and life in it; therefore, it is still quite pertinent to ask if things are as old as evolutionists claim.

Many telling attacks can be launched against the various methods of geochronology based on radiometric dating methods. Some of the very basic assumptions of these methods, such as steady-state existence of C-14 in the atmosphere, constancy of decay rates in the long radiological clocks, etc., seem to be erroneous.[2] I will limit the present paper, however, to presenting several indicators which imply a rather short age for the Solar System. In pointing these out, I will follow the thinking of the scheme which is the basis of any dating system, namely: the measurement of some physical quantity (Q) produced in the time associated with some event, the determination of the rate (R) at which this quantity is produced, and, consequently, the calculation of the time (T) involved in the production of the quantity, and, thus, the dating of the past event, where:

$$T = Q/R$$

Cosmic Dust Influx

The first of these indicators has to do with the influx of meteoric dust into the earth's atmosphere from inter-planetary space and finally down onto the earth's surface and eventually into the oceans. This dust material is called micrometeoric since the particles are obviously very small, being only a few ten thousandths of a centimeter in diameter. These particles are moving so slowly that they do not burn up with entry into the atmosphere and they settle very gradually to the earth's surface.

The material may be collected in chemical trays, and then analyzed as to what is extra-terrestrial. Only the mass of the magnetic meteoric material is used in the calculations, since stony meteoric matter cannot be clearly separated from terrestrial matter. Consequently, esti-mates of the influx of meteoric dust are very conservative by chemical methods since stony meteorites are considered far more abundant than iron meteorites. By studying satellite impacts with the micrometeorites, a count of the number of particles, the size distribution of the particles, and the mass of these particles can be made. This gives a more reliable determination than the chemical-tray-collector approach.

Estimates of the influx range considerably with different investigators. The Swedish geophysicist, Petter-son, estimates 14,300,000 tons of meteoric dust come onto the surface of the earth per year.[3] In five billion years there should be a layer of dust approximately 54 feet in thickness on the earth if it were to lie undisturbed without our erosional agents acting on it. Since the erosional agents are acting, tremendous amounts of nickel (since it is one of the major constituents of meteorites) should be carried into the oceans.

Nickel, on the other hand, is actually a rare element in terrestrial rocks and continental sediments and is nearly non-existent in ocean water and ocean sediments. This seems to indicate a very short age for oceans. Taking the amount of nickel in the ocean water and ocean sediments and using the rate at which nickel is being added to the water from meteoric material, the length of time of accumulation turns out to be only several thousand years, rather than a few billion years.

From core samples of deep sea sediments, there is a near absence of the cosmic spherules (cosmic dust that has been shaped on travel through the atmosphere) from interplanetary space, but quite an abundance of meteorite ablation products (material produced in the destruction of a meteor as it travels through the air), relatively speaking. This would indicate that the ocean sediments are young.

From the reports of the first lunar landing, the accumulation of dust on the surface of the moon in the vicinity of the touch-down was very small (not much more than 1/8").[4] The following landings were in "seas" that had larger dust accumulations, but still very small in thickness. The moon moves through the same region of space that the earth does, and, consequently, should have about the same influx of cosmic dust as the earth. Astronomers were worried that a lunar ship would sink down into the supposed huge amount of dust that should have accumulated on the surface in about 4.5 billion years of assumed time.

Also, in the "sea" areas, where the lunar ships landed, there should have accumulated more dust than elsewhere on the moon. Yet, the amount of dust is amazingly small. What could have happened to all the dust?

Although more data and calculations are needed to make a quantitative study of the moon's age on this basis, from the absence of dust, we may deduce a short period of time for accumulation, and, thus, a young age for the moon. If the earth is about the same age as the moon (as the Scriptures assert and as most astronomers believe), then the earth must also be young.

Poynting-Robertson Effect

A second indicator of youth (low entropy state) is given by the Poynting-Robertson effect. Solar radiation has an important influence on the orbits of small particles which have a large ratio of surface area to mass. Several points of consideration are significant.

First, there is a simple outward force from the sun due to radiation pressure. For particles with diameters of a few thousand angstroms

$$(1A^\circ = 10^{-8}cm = 1/100,000,000cm)$$

or less, this force may exceed the gravitational attraction of the sun and blow them out of the Solar System.

Second, the solar radiation received by a particle is Doppler-shifted to cause an increase in radiation pressure if the particle is approaching the sun, and a decrease if it is receding; thus, changing elliptical orbits to circular ones.

Third, the angular momentum of an orbiting particle is progressively destroyed since it receives solar radiation, which has only a radial momentum from the sun, and re-radiates this energy with a forward momentum corresponding to its own motion about the sun. This produces a drag force on the particle causing it to spiral into the sun. This is called the Poynting-Robertson effect. Robertson[5] found that a particle of rock (density 2.7) one centimeter in diameter started at the earth's distance would fall into the sun in 10 million years. In a time of 2 billion years, any masses of rock less than six feet in diameter within the earth's orbit would be cast into the sun. This "sweeping up" process would get rid of anything less than three inches in diameter inside Jupiter's orbit, and anything less than 1/10 inch in diameter inside Neptune's orbit. Yet, significant quantities of meteoric matter are known to exist! There is the huge cloud of particles grouped around the sun which reflect sunlight called the zodiacal cloud. A tremendous amount of matter is there!

THE AGE OF THE SOLAR SYSTEM
(PART II)

Age of Comets Calculated

As comets travel around the sun, they are continually undergoing disintegration from gravitational and radiative effects of the sun and planets. This phenomenon may be taken as a third indication of young age of the Solar System.

Comets have been observed to diminish in size and even to break up. Debris for meteor showers remains along their orbits. Comets are generally of two types: short-period and long-period. Most astronomers believe that the comets and the planets came into existence about the same time. If this is true and the lifetime of a comet can be estimated, the age of the planets can then be determined.

The German astronomer, Swinne, estimates the maximum life of a short-period comet is 25,000 years. Lyttleton estimates that no short-period comet can survive longer than approximately 10,000 years.[6] Considering the "dynamical" effects of the planets in causing the long-period comets to be ejected from the solar system, Lyttleton estimates that only one in 10,000 could be left after 4.5 billion years. This does not take into account physical disruption of the comet which would further reduce this estimate.

Calculation of a short life for comets has led to a number of hypotheses to explain away the obvious, that the Solar System is young. These attempts have ranged all the way from ejections of comets by volcanic action from the planet Jupiter to comets coming from the galaxy outside the Solar System. Certain astronomers have also suggested that there is something akin to a "deep-freeze" storage of comets 13,950,000,000 miles from the sun, which is continually replenishing the supply of comets to the Solar System. Needless to say, this alleged shell of comets cannot be seen with the telescope.

These many hypotheses have been made to avoid the notion of youth for the Solar System, but as yet there is no real evidence for any of these pseudo-scientific ideas. Had the age turned out rather large by this method, however, I think the evolutionists would have welcomed the results without question! Lyttleton makes the comment:

> "In the whole age of this system, a comet with average period 100,000 years would make 4.5×10^4 returns to the sun, and if at each one of these it lost only 1/1000 of its mass, through tail-formation and meteor stream production, the initial mass would have been more than 10^{19} times as great as the present mass — which at a minimum means several times the mass of the sun."[7]

When one adopts a naturalistic explanation of origins, he is soon driven to incredible extremes!

Other Indicators of Youth

There are other indicators for a young age in general, such as the destruction of the spiral arms of the galaxies due to differential rotation. Stars and gas in a galaxy rotate in Keplerian orbits where the velocity decreases outward from the center of the galaxy. This causes a winding up of the spiral arms in a short time (relatively speaking). It is believed by some that the magnetic field maintains the coherence of the arms. However, the strength of the field seems rather small and not nearly strong enough to maintain the galactic arms. Also, there is the rapid break-up of the star clusters which at most takes only several thousand years in many cases. The helium content of the atmosphere is yet another interesting sign pointing to young age of the earth. Helium content of the atmosphere, its exudation rate from the lithosphere, and other considerations indicate a maximum atmospheric age of around 10,000 to 100,000 years.[8]

These are a few of the signs pointing to a young age of the earth and the Solar System. Much excellent work with regard to the age of the earth has been done already by Dr. Melvin A. Cook concerning the radiological "clocks" and is reported in the above reference. His work indicates that these clocks, too, may give very small ages for geological events when all external influencing factors are considered.

References (Part I)

1. Blum, Harold F. 1955. *Time's Arrow and Evolution.* Second Edition, Princeton University Press, Princeton, New Jersey.
2. Slusher, Harold S. 1973. *A Critique of Radiometric Dating Methods*, Institute for Creation Research, San Diego, California.
3. Petterson, H. 1960. Cosmic Spherules and Meteoric Dust. *Scientific American*, 202:132. February.
4. *El Paso Herald-Post*, July 21, 1969.
5. Robertson, H.P. 1937. Dynamical Effects of Radiation in the Solar System. *N.R.A.S.*, April, 1937.

References (Part II)

6. Lyttleton, R.A. 1968. *Mysteries of the Solar System.* Clarendon Press, Oxford, England, p. 110.
7. *Ibid.*, p. 147.
8. Cook, Melvin A. 1966. *Prehistory and Earth Models.* Max Parish and Co., Ltd., London, p. 14.

I.C.R. WELCOMES NEW DIRECTOR OF DEVELOPMENT

We are happy to welcome Mr. David E. Harris to the staff of I.C.R. Mr. Harris, an alumnus of Ontario Bible College in Toronto, will be serving as the Director of Development. If you would like his assistance in some area of estate planning or other areas of Christian stewardship, he would be happy to be of help. Just write to him in care of I.C.R.

NEW ZEALAND RECEIVES UNIQUE
EXPOSURE TO CREATIONISM

What has undoubtedly been the most extensive coverage in history of a single nation with the message of scientific Biblical creationism has just been completed in New Zealand by Dr. Henry Morris, Director of I.C.R. In five weeks, July 4 — August 8, Dr. Morris averaged five speaking assignments daily for 35 days, covering all the major cities and universities, as well as numerous high schools, churches, and other groups.

News media gave extensive coverage to the meetings, including appearances on New Zealand's national radio and television networks. Interest was high in all meetings, with total attendance of nearly 18,000 people, not including those who tuned in on the eight radio and T.V. broadcasts.

New Zealand's schools have been completely secularized for many decades and evolution is taught exclusively everywhere, even in church schools. Dr. Morris lectured on creationism to students in 23 public high schools, 11 Roman Catholic high schools, and 4 other church high schools.

A total of 23 meetings were held on the five major university campuses of the country (Auckland, Victoria, Otago, Canterbury, and Waitaka Universities) and four teachers' colleges. The largest single attendance was 1,500 students who came to hear the debate at Auckland University between Dr. Morris and Dr. C. Loring Brace, Visiting Professor from the University of Michigan and one of the world's leading evolutionary anthropologists. Faculty attendance was also high at most campus meetings.

The lecture tour was set up and sponsored by the New Zealand Evangelical Alliance. Tony Hanne, M.D., Director of the Capernwray Bible Institute in Auckland, and Gordon Brown, B.A. (Anthropology, Auckland University), Traveling Secretary for the Alliance, were in charge of the arrangements and will be acting also as I.C.R. contacts in New Zealand for future distribution of creationist literature in their country, as well as for promotion of future creationist meetings and activities there.

READERS' COMMENTS

"I am teaching a course in Physical Anthropology to high school students in September, and since I am a born again Christian, I am most concerned about presenting a course like this carefully . . . I praise God that your broadcast (Science, Scripture, and Salvation) came when I was most troubled about teaching this new course!"

M.P., New Jersey

"Would you please send us today's transcript on 'Scientists Who Believe in the Bible' . . . We are so glad there are great men that believe in the Bible and not just all simple people like myself.　　　　H.K., Ohio

"It may interest you to know that your fine literature is given to men of the sea, of the many unbelievers. Your literature gives them an opportunity to stop and reconsider their standing before our Lord and Saviour Jesus Christ. Thank you for ICR ACTS & FACTS."

G.B., New York

"Enclosed is a small gift for the unique and important work you are engaged in. As a high school science teacher, I consider your informative publications a boon to Christian educators."　　　　R.C., Pennsylvania

"Just want to let you know how much I enjoy your program, 'Science, Scripture, and Salvation,' as I listen each Saturday morning over Family Radio . . . Hope you can keep your fine program coming our way until Jesus comes."　　　　D.S., California

"I appreciate what you're doing and enjoy the information that comes in the mail. Keep up the good work."　　　　H.S., Maryland

"I also want to say what a blessing I.C.R. has been to my life. Anyone could scientifically come up with the same evidences for Creation you have who is a Christian, but I've never heard such a fundamental evangelical balance of scripture that I.C.R. presents as a result of the evidences which are established. I pray that the close adherence to God's word will always be there and that the world might be changed by recognizing who their Creator and Saviour is . . . I praise God for your stand firmly on God's Word."   P.T., New Jersey

"Thank you for sending to me each issue of ACTS & FACTS. I find it extremely interesting to read a science-oriented magazine that supports the Bible."
                                                                    J.H., Washington

DIRECTOR'S COLUMN
Henry M. Morris, Pd.D.

An exciting summer is almost over now and we are looking forward to an even more exciting fall. I have just returned from spending most of the summer in the middle of the winter, filling a total of 180 speaking assignments in New Zealand, Australia, and New Guinea in a six-week period. Everywhere the interest in scientific Biblical creationism seems high and going higher. Duane Gish, Harold Slusher, and others have been busy in our five Summer Institutes, and they report the same.

The Ararat project encountered impenetrable political barriers this summer, and the I.C.R. expedition had to be content with archaeological and topographical surveys in the vicinity of the mountain. Even so, however, there were numerous evidences of the Lord's leading in various circumstances, and important contacts were made with good prospects for the future.

There are so many demands on our scientific staff for speaking — many of which are so strategic that we feel we must accept them if possible — that our textbook progress has been slower than hoped. However, we now have two new books about ready to go to press, and we anticipate their publication late this fall. One is our long-awaited high school textbook on world history, STREAMS OF CIVILIZATION, by Albert Hyma and

Mary Stanton. The other is a comprehensive textbook on practical Christian evidences, tentatively entitled LET GOD BE TRUE, which has been developed over the past three years for our course in that subject here at Christian Heritage College. A third important new book, of multiple authorship, is almost complete, consisting of a comprehensive and authoritative, yet understandable, handbook on all aspects of scientific creationism. We believe each of these books will fill a vital need in the Christian world.

Space does not allow me to discuss other plans for the fall, including addresses on many important university campuses and at scientific meetings These will be reported from time to time in ACTS & FACTS. The schedule is heavy and we trust God will supply all needed strength and grace. We are thrilled and grateful to watch Him work in such unusual ways these days.

1,500 ATTEND DEBATE AT VAN NUYS

Approximately 1,500 people, most of them college students, attended the debate on "Creation versus Evolution" recently held at the First Baptist Church of Van Nuys, California, between two biologists from the University of Southern California, Dr. David Morafka and Dr. William T. O'Day, defending evolution, and Dr. Duane Gish and Dr. Henry Morris, of I.C.R., speaking for creation. Interest was high and almost all the audience stayed not only throughout the two-hour debate, but also for the open question-and-answer session following.

The debate was the feature event of a week-long Creation Seminar held in connection with the National Youth Strategy Conference sponsored by the church and the Van Nuys Christian College. To begin the seminar, Dr. Morris spoke at both morning services of the church, which is recognized as the largest church in the West. About 4,000 were in attendance at the two services. Two sessions were held each night, Monday through Friday, with the debate on Wednesday. Approximately 1,000 attended each regular evening session.

Speakers also included Harold Slusher and John Morris, and the film "Footprints in Stone" was shown as well. Both Dr. Harold Fickett, pastor of the church, and David Nicholas, Dean of the College, were enthusiastic in their evaluation of the impact of the meetings on the lives of hundreds of young people throughout the San Fernando Valley.

CAP PROGRAM BRINGS
GREAT RESPONSE

In the May, 1973 issue of ACTS & FACTS, an article was featured about the CAP Program (College Ad Project). This project was conceived and initially sponsored by an insurance executive who had a strong desire to reach college students on the secular campus with the fact that special creation is a more viable and logical explanation of origins than the molecules-to-man theory of evolution. A three-part series of mind-provoking, eye-appealing advertisements was prepared by I.C.R. scientists and published in several college newspapers just before the summer vacation. As previously reported, the response was excellent.

Many readers have inquired as to how to sponsor a similar program on college campuses in their own areas. The procedure, briefly, is as follows: each sponsor designates the campus or campuses he wishes to reach, and I.C.R. places the series of ads in the college papers, furnishing photo-ready copy to the papers. The sponsor is then sent information each month about the costs involved (approximately 40¢ per student response for materials sent the student, plus the cost of ad insertions), and he sends I.C.R. a tax-deductible gift in that amount.

Since the advertisements emphasize "no strings attached" — and thereby intimate that no one will contact them — I.C.R. does not furnish the names and addresses

90

of the inquirers to the sponsor. However, if the student is sufficiently interested to inquire a second time for the second packet of info (which includes the booklet, *God's Plan for Your Life*), names and addresses will then be made available to sponsoring churches or campus organizations for additional follow-up if they request this information.

The enthusiastic response already noted, both by students and by readers of ACTS & FACTS, indicates the CAP Program to be an effective way of reaching hundreds of campuses across the nation. Since I.C.R. funds are very limited, however, specific sponsors are necessary for each campus on which the ads appear.

CREATION MESSAGE
GIVEN IN AUSTRALIA
AND NEW GUINEA

. . . I.C.R. extended its teaching ministry to the most distant points yet when Dr. Henry Morris lectured during late August to audiences in Brisbane, Australia, and Ukarumpa, New Guinea. The meeting in Brisbane was sponsored by the Australia branch of the Evolution Protest Movement and was held in the Central Baptist Church, a 117-year-old church in the heart of the city, with approximately 300 in attendance. Dr. Morris was in Australia overnight, enroute to New Guinea after his five-week lecture tour of New Zealand.

Ukarumpa, in the eastern highlands of Papua-New Guinea, is the headquarters of the New Guinea Branch of the Wycliffe Bible Translators and the Summer Institute of Linguistics, with about 400 missionary linguists and support workers centered there. Dr. and Mrs. Morris spent ten days visiting their daughter and son-in-law, Mr. & Mrs. Les Bruce, who are working with the Alamblak people along the Kariwari River in northwestern New Guinea. While in Ukarumpa, Dr. Morris gave four lectures on scientific creationism to the S.I.L. staff and the students in the S.I.L. high school. The importance of a creationist approach in their linguistic and anthropological studies was stressed.

INSTRUCTION IN TEXTBOOK ADOPTION PROCEDURES AVAILABLE

Among the many inquiries received at I.C.R. each day, one of the most frequent is for information and assistance in getting into the school systems textbooks that give equal emphasis to the scientific creation position on the theory of origins.

The major function of the Institute is research, textbook writing, and lecturing on the subject of creationism on campuses, churches, at seminars, etc.; and even though we have written several useful articles in the ACTS & FACTS and other brief papers dealing with this problem, in many cases we have been unable to give these sincere requests the individual and personal attention whch we feel they deserve.

We recently were very pleased to receive news that the Mel Gablers, who have been working in this area privately for a number of years, have felt the call of God to take an early retirement and devote full time to this effort. Mel and Norma Gabler are widely known for their studies of new textbooks and for their writing and speaking throughout Texas and the nation, urging parents to be more alert and active in the selection of books to be used by school children. Mr. Gabler says, "Now is the time for others to do more in this vital battle for the minds of children, because our nation moves in the exact direction children are taught. Parents must join in doing what individuals and groups across our nation have started doing already to correct this situation."

Toward this end, the Gablers have formed a non-profit organization called, "Educational Research Analysts", and have offered helpful information to those who request it by writing to P.O. Box 7175, Longview, Texas 75601.

1973 SUMMER INSTITUTE "WRAP-UP"

The Institute for Creation Research conducted week-long institutes on Biblical and scientific creationism during the summer at San Diego; Springfield, Missouri (Evangel College); Lynchburg, Virginia (Lynchburg Baptist College); Olds, Alberta; and Seattle (Northwest College).

These summer institutes reached a very strategic group of people, including many teachers, college students, and pastors. Included among enrollees this summer, for example, were school board members, a Bible college president, and a science coordinator with over 60 public school science teachers under him.

Students attending the institutes were almost universal in their praise of the benefits they had received from the institute they attended. Near the conclusion of the institute at Olds, Alberta, one of the students, a college graduate, reported to Dr. Gish and Prof. Slusher that he had almost abandoned his faith as the result of his experience at college, but, having been tremendously strengthened in his faith, his attendance at the institute represented a big turning point in his life.

Faculty for the institutes included Dr. Duane Gish and Professor Harold Slusher (all five institutes), Dr. Henry Morris (Springfield), Dr. Robert Franks and Stuart Nevins (San Diego), Dr. John N. Moore (Lynchburg and Seattle), and Dr. George Howe (Olds).

Five institutes are tentatively planned through the United States for the summer of 1974. Dates and locations will be announced about the first of the year. Why not plan right now to set aside one week next summer for this valuable training? If desired, two units college credit, either undergraduate or graduate, are granted for attending these institutes. Graduate credits through Azusa Pacific College.

DIRECTOR'S COLUMN
Henry M. Morris, Ph.D.

One of the most encouraging trends that we have noted the last year or two is the spiritual vitality of the young people, and especially their interest in creationism. Dr. Gish and I have spoken on over forty college and university campuses within the past year and have always found a courteous hearing and intense interest from large numbers of students. We have been in even a greater number of high schools, and the same has been true there. The very few instances of rudeness we have encountered have been from faculty members, not students!

Similarly, in our Seminars and creation conferences in churches, it is nearly always the case that the majority of the audience is composed of students and young married adults. Whatever may be the reason for this phenomenon — disillusion with the scientific and compromising religious establishments, the "Jesus Movement" revivals, a pendulum-swing reaction from the student radicalism of the past decade, or whatever — in any case, these students in large numbers are showing great interest in creationism. As a further, more concrete, example, I believe the present group of students enrolled at Christian Heritage College is the finest group of young people I have met in over thirty years of college teaching! I hope every one of our readers can visit us soon, not only to see our beautiful new campus, but also to meet our students.

I believe it was Charles Clough (who is both a scientist and pastor) who first called my attention to a most remarkable fact. The interest in creationism today seems largely to be centered in the young and in the old. Those in the retirement-age brackets, like the younger generation, seem to be thrilled at today's revival of creationism. This fact is reflected both in our mail and in our public meetings.

But there is a serious generation gap! The age range from about 35 to 60 (my own generation, in fact) has been the most difficult to reach. This generation constitutes the "establishment"; it is the generation marked by the great depression and by World War II and its aftermath. More than any other generation, it is thoroughly indoctrinated in evolutionism and materialism. The religious leaders of this generation have been largely committed to neo-orthodoxy or neo-evangelicalism.

While we are thankful for the response of the older generation and excited at the interest of the younger generation, somehow we also need to reach this middle generation! By and large, these are the ones in positions of greatest influence, the ones who could, if they would, also provide the critically-needed financing for creationist textbooks and research and education. Pray for them.

GENESIS SCHOOL OF GRADUATE STUDIES

The first known post-graduate level college stressing scientific creationism in its degree programs opened its doors with the 1973-74 academic year. The Genesis School of Graduate Studies, located in Gainesville, Florida (home of the University of Florida), will offer master's and doctor's degrees in several fields, including Education, Communications, and Science/Creation Research. All curricula will stress special creation and the young earth model. Areas of scientific emphasis include biochemistry and biostatistics.

The Genesis School will work in close cooperation with Christian Heritage College and the Institute for Creation Research. Professors Henry Morris, Duane Gish, and Harold Slusher of Christian Heritage College are listed as Adjunct Professors at the Genesis School, and I.C.R. opened the educational program there on September 21-24 with an intensive Seminar on Scientific Creationism.

Carl F. George, M.A., is President of the new college. He is also pastor of Gainesville's University Baptist Church, whose facilities will be shared with the College. Craig H. Lampe, with a Ph.D. in Biochemistry from the University of Florida, is Vice-President. Jack C. Summers (Ph.D., Chemistry, University of Florida) is Dean of Administration, and Donald F. Clark (Ph.D., Chemistry, University of Florida) is Academic Dean.

ARARAT
REPORT

Mount Ararat has resisted successfully once again. The I.C.R. expedition, as well as a number of others, spent several weeks in Turkey during the summer in an attempt to reach Noah's Ark, but were thwarted as the Kurdish curtain held once more.

The I.C.R. team, led by John Morris, was prepared through glacier training on Mount Rainier, the Turkish summer was unusually warm, and all the other signs were favorable, except one. The political barrier, despite many and varied approaches, proved impenetrable, for reasons unknown, and permits to climb Mount Ararat could not be obtained. However, an extensive telephoto survey was made of the upper slopes of Mount Ararat and these photographs are now being studied.

Despite these setbacks, the I.C.R. team made a number of important contacts which it is believed may lead to governmental cooperation next year. In view of all past evidences of the Ark's preservation, and the tremendous impact its full discovery would have, it is believed that the project should be continued either until the Ark is finally located or until it becomes certain that it has not been preserved after all.

CHRISTIAN HERITAGE BEGINS FOURTH YEAR

On its beautiful new El Cajon campus for the first time, Christian Heritage College has begun its fourth year of operation with a record enrollment of 130 students, including over 100 full-time students. The new freshman class is not only more than twice as large as the 1972 freshman enrollment, but is composed of young men and women of unusually high intellectual and spiritual calibre.

Approximately 40% of the students are from outside the San Diego metropolitan area. Students have come from 8 states other than California (Michigan, Alabama, Louisiana, Oregon, New Mexico, Florida, Washington, Texas), as well as Mexico and Japan.

The unusually large percentage of students from outside San Diego, especially for such a young college, reflects the growing national awareness of the unique educational environment and programs at Christian Heritage.

GISH DEBATES CUFFEY AT PENN STATE

Over 1500 students and faculty members were in attendance on the night of October 10, when Dr. Duane T. Gish, Associate Director of the Institute for Creation Research, engaged Dr. Roger Cuffey in a debate on creation versus evolution. Although, in accordance with the custom in such debates, no formal vote was taken, general student reaction indicated that Gish's arguments and evidence were more cogent and persuasive than those of the evolutionist. The student organization sponsoring the debate, the Overcomers, is attempting to follow up on a personal basis the large number of students who expressed interest in knowing more about creationism and Christianity.

Dr. Roger J. Cuffey, who debated Dr. Gish, is a Professor of Paleontology in the Department of Geosciences at Penn State. He is well-known as a leader in the American Scientific Affiliation, serving as its Consulting Editor in Paleontology, and is an outspoken critic of the position on special creaton and flood geology advocated by the Institute for Creation Research. The debate provided an ideal opportunity for students to hear both sides of the issue from two of the leaders on each side.

Most of Cuffey's arguments centered on his contention that the fossil record proved evolution, including the evolutionary origin of man. Dr. Gish, however, showed conclusively that Dr. Cuffey's supposed "transitional forms" were either invalid or irrelevant. Further, he showed that evolution was precluded by the Second Law of Thermodynamics, an argument which was not answered, either by Dr. Cuffey or the many Penn State faculty members who spoke during the question-and-answer session following the debate. This fact, reinforced by the absence of any evidence for present-day upward evolutionary change, and the systematic absence of incipient and transitional forms in the fossil record, makes the evolutionary model look extremely weak when compared on a scientific basis with the creation model. Evolution must be "believed" as an article of humanistic faith, but it was obvious from Dr. Gish's arguments that it had no basis in genuine science.

MEYER A NEW MEMBER OF I.C.R.
ADVISORY BOARD

The newest member of the Technical Advisory Board of the Institute for Creation Research is Dr. John R. Meyer. Dr. Meyer is Assistant Professor of Physiology and Biophysics at the University of Louisville. Dr. Meyer has an unusual educational background, with a B.A. in Bible from Faith Baptist Bible College in Iowa, followed by a B.A. in Chemistry from Kearney State College in Nebraska, and a Ph.D. in Zoology from the University of Iowa. He also studied at Omaha University and Duke University, and served four years as a Postdoctoral Research Fellow at the Cardiovascular Pulmonary Research Center at the University of Colorado.

Dr. Meyer is an active Baptist layman and an excellent and experienced speaker on Bible-science subjects. Churches and other organizations in the eastern states needing a speaker should consider inviting him.

CREATIONIST INTEREST CONTINUES IN NEW ZEALAND

Reports coming from New Zealand indicate that the influence of Dr. Henry Morris' tour there during July and August is still bearing fruit.

A letter from Dr. Tony Hanne, of the Evangelical Alliance, which sponsored the tour, indicates that orders for tapes of the messages given in Auckland are being received in substantial numbers. Tentative plans are under way for a similar tour, perhaps next year, by Dr. Duane Gish.

The Brethren Assemblies of New Zealand (approximately 250 in number) are making plans to send copies of Dr. Morris' book *The Remarkable Birth of Planet Earth* to all the families in their churches requesting it. The intent of this distribution is to help counteract the influence of Professor Robert Boyd, a prominent scientist in England and a member of one of the Brethren Assemblies there, whose advocacy of theistic evolution is having considerable influence among their churches. Professor Boyd was on a similar lecture tour through New Zealand at the same time Dr. Morris was there last summer.

READERS' COMMENTS

"Let me say that I have enjoyed the books and I would appreciate it if you would pass along a complement to Dr. Morris for me saying that I have extremely enjoyed the ICR Impact Series. Keep up the work and Praise the Lord!"

V.M., Texas

"I am very pleased with the articles you publish in your ICR ACTS & FACTS. They have been very helpful in presenting material to my campus-career class at church and my sixth grade class in which I teach at school. I have many opportunities to use them as resource material in defending special creation attacks."

J.Z., Florida

"It's quite refreshing to hear such a sound, Scriptural position in relation to the Bible and science — true science, that is . . . I appreciate your stand in the face of such wide-spread so-called scientific theories that are predominant today. Keep up the good work."

A.P., Washington

"Thank you for the ACTS & FACTS and other material you have sent . . . You will find that the Creation vs. Evolution controversy will play a most important part in the crises that will close the history of this troubled world."

F.B., California

"Just a line to tell you I listen each Saturday to your program. . . I find it to be very true to the Bible Scriptures and also very beneficial to my everyday encounters with other people as I go through this life here on earth."

A.H., New Jersey

"I deeply appreciate all you are doing and find your materials most helpful."

Rev. D.P., Indiana

"I wish to receive your ACTS & FACTS. I find it a great blessing and has convinced me of the truth of creation. I am a graduate student in microbiology and as a scientist find your monthly letter great. Thank you and keep up the great work you are doing."

D.M., New Mexico

"I would very much appreciate receiving a copy of this morning's discussion as I am sure it would be very helpful to some students I know who have had only the Evolutionary Theory of Creation taught to them. Thank you for these fine broadcasts each Saturday morning — they are very helpful in showing the false theories that have led our children astray because this is the only side they are hearing these days. Truly false teachers are now everywhere in our educational systems."

G.N., Maryland

"I've read many of your books and think they're great! Thanks."

C.R., Florida

"I could not repress a smile when I thought of the consternation it will cause in our Centers of Learning where the views of skeptical professors dominate. May I give you my ABSOLUTE confidence in your sincere efforts to overcome the gigantic opposition which naturally confronts all those who embark on a project of such import."

C.G., Derbyshire, England

"A group of fellow Christians and myself are in the initial stages of opening a Christian Coffeehouse. We wish to open as one of the outreach services connected with it a Christian street library. Since many non-Christians are enslaved with Mid-Victorian Darwinianisms in their approach patterns to God's Airport of Jesus International it would be a blessing to have the fruits of your searchings to present to them. It is such a strong and potent revelation that God and Science are not hostile combatants in the lawful deed to this Universe."

T.B., Wisconsin

"I would also like to express my appreciation for the work you are doing. I believe in creation, yet I was confused about the so-called proof for evolution. We had a speaker at camp. His name was Dr. Chittick and he spoke on creation. It is good to know that there is proof of the Biblical account of creation. Thank you again.

C.W., Washington

2200 HEAR CREATION MESSAGE
AT SPURGEON'S TABERNACLE IN LONDON

At a gathering of Baptists unprecedented in England since the days of Charles Haddon Spurgeon, Dr. Henry Morris, Director of the Institute for Creation Research, spoke on "The Twilight of Evolution" to 2200 delegates and visitors to the International Congress of Fundamental Baptist Churches, on November 6 in the large Metropolitan Tabernacle in London, England. His message emphasized the scientific superiority of the creation model of origins over the evolution model, showing: (1) evolution across the created kinds does not occur at present; (2) the fossil record shows evolution did not occur in the past; (3) evolution could not occur at all, because of the restrictions imposed by the second law of thermodynamics; (4) even if evolution were conceivable, there has not been nearly enough time, as shown especially by radio-carbon dating of the atmosphere and magnetic field strength dating of the earth's core.

Dr. Morris spoke at the Wednesday-night session of the five-day Congress, the first such international meeting of fundamental Baptists ever held, so far as known. Baptists from at least 18 countries attended the Congress, with the largest delegation coming from the United States. The meeting place was uniquely appropriate, as the Metropolitan Tabernacle was made famous during the 19th century by its Pastor Spurgeon, considered by most Baptists to be the greatest Baptist preacher of modern times.

The emphasis on a return to literal creationism was apparently warmly endorsed by the large audience, as indicated by a spontaneous ovation at its conclusion, the only such demonstration of the Congress. It is hoped that the effects will be felt in hundreds of churches around the world.

BRITISH SCIENTISTS FORM
CREATIONIST ORGANIZATION

At a meeting held in London's Metropolitan Tabernacle on November 6, 1973, about 20 creationist scientists in the London area laid tentative plans for a British Society to oppose evolution in the United Kingdom. Under the temporary chairmanship of geographer-geologist Edgar C. Powell, the society will probably be called the Newton Scientific Association and will stress scientific, rather than religious, difficulties with evolution, hoping to make significant contributions to the subject in British scientific journals.

103

The meeting was held at a dinner preceding the address by Dr. Henry Morris, reported elsewhere in this issue of *Acts & Facts*, to the International Congress of Fundamental Baptist Churches. After the discussion concerning the proposed organization, Dr. Morris reviewed the history of creationism in the United States, discussing especially the various science-oriented Christian organizations. The Newton Scientific Association will not be affiliated with any other organization, but will try to design its program to meet the unique needs of Great Britain itself.

WORD-OF-LIFE CONFERENCE

Dr. Henry Morris was the featured speaker at the Annual Pastor's Conference at the Word-of-Life Conference Grounds on beautiful Schroon Lake in upstate New York. The Director of the Conference, as well as of all the varied Word-of-Life ministries, Jack Wyrtzen, expressed warm appreciation of the messages and of the ICR program. Pastors from at least eight of the northeastern states were present at the conference.

Dr. Morris also spoke to four special joint-class sessions of the 250-plus students at the Word-of-Life Bible Institute, all of whom are in an intensive one-year Bible curriculum. Many of the students expressed an intention to continue their education at Christian Heritage College next year. The student body showed an unusual appreciation for the creationism lectures by a spontaneous standing ovation at the conclusion of the last session.

REPRINT

'MAN'S UNIQUE'
EVOLUTION NOT A FACT,
SAYS PROFESSOR
From the Chicago Daily News

CHICAGO — An Indiana professor of anthropology has critized his colleagues sharply for declaring "as fact" that man descended from apelike creatures.

Prof. Anthony Ostric of St. Mary's College, South Bend, said that at best the ape theory is only a hypothesis and not a well-supported one at that.

The Darwinian evolutionary theory has been promoted by only a few leaders in anthropology and human biology, Ostric declared, but, he said, the vast body of professionals have fallen in behind them "for fear of not being declared serious scholars or of being rejected from serious academic circles."

Ostric told the ninth International Congress of Anthropological and Ethnological Sciences here that there was no evidence that man had not remained essentially the same since the first evidence of his appearance.

A hundred thousand years ago man began to assume a dominant role and less than 20,000 years ago became fully dominant as his brain enlarged to about its present size.

There is no compelling evidence to support this picture, Ostric said. As for the brain, the Neanderthal man's was at least as large as that of the most modern races. In weight of brain in proportion to the weight of body, the marmoset, the dwarf monkey of South America, surpasses man.

The key to the secret doorway through which man came into the world is unknown, Ostric said.

The theory of evolution holds that all things that have ever lived began with a single organic beginning in the seas, moved to land and that through the process of mutation and radiation, all things differentiated.

Man's ancestors supposedly descended from trees where they had swung from branch to branch. On the ground, they adopted an erect posture, used their forearms to make tools, discovered fire, developed carnivorous habits and began developing a brain — all of this more than a half-million years ago.

"To say there were pre-human ape ancestors transformed into humans is speculative," he asserted.

"Man's unique biophysical and socio-cultural nature appears now to represent an unbridgeable abyss separating him from all other animals, even from his closest 'anthropoid relatives.'

"It is not possible to see how biological, social or cultural forces or processes could transform any kind of prehuman anthropoid or 'near-man' into homo sapiens."

IMPACT SERIES

NO. 1 THROUGH NO. 9

"VITAL ARTICLES ON SCIENCE/CREATION"
INSTITUTE FOR CREATION RESEARCH

EVOLUTION, CREATION AND
THE PUBLIC SCHOOLS
Henry M. Morris, Ph.D.

One of the most amazing phenomena in the history of education is that a speculative philosophy based on no true scientific evidence could have been universally adopted and taught as scientific fact, in all the public schools. This philosophy has been made the very framework of modern education and the underlying premise in all textbooks. It constitutes the present world-view of liberal intellectuals in every field.

This is the philosophy of evolution. Although widely promoted as a scientific fact, evolution has never been proved scientifically. Some writers still call it the *theory* of evolution, but even this is too generous. A scientific hypothesis should be capable of being tested in some way, to determine whether or not it is true, but evolution cannot be tested. No laboratory experiment can either confirm or falsify a process which, by its very nature, requires millions of years to accomplish significant results.

Evolution is, therefore, neither fact, theory, nor hypothesis. It is a belief — and nothing more.

When creationists propose, however, that creation be taught in the schools along with evolution, evolutionists commonly react emotionally, rather than scientifically. Their "religion" of naturalism and humanism has been in effect the established religion of the state for a hundred years, and they fear competition.

In the present world, neither evolution nor creation is taking place, so far as can be observed (and *science* is supposed to be based on observation!). Cats beget cats and fruit-flies beget fruit-flies. Life comes only from life. There is nothing new under the sun.

Neither evolution nor creation is accessible to the scientific method, since they deal with origins and history, not with presently observable and repeatable events. They can, however, be formulated as scientific *models*, or frameworks, within which to predict and correlate observed facts. Neither can be *proved*; neither can be *tested*. They can only be *compared* in terms of the relative ease with which they can explain data which exist in the real world.

There are, therefore, sound scientific and pedagogical reasons why *both* models should be taught, as objectively as possible, in public classrooms, giving arguments pro and con for each. Some students and their parents believe in creation, some in evolution, and some are undecided. If creationists desire *only* the creation model to be taught, they should send their children to private schools which do this; if evolutionists want only evolution to be taught, they should provide private schools for *that* purpose. The public schools should be neutral and either teach both or teach neither.

This is clearly the most equitable and constitutional approach. Many people have been led to believe, however, that court decisions restricting "religious" teaching in the public schools apply to "creation" teaching and not to "evolution" teaching. Nevertheless, creationism is actually a far more effective scientific model than evolutionism, and evolution requires a far more credulous religious faith in the illogical and unproveable than does creation. An abundance of sound scientific literature is available today to document this statement, but few evolutionists have bothered to read any of it. Many of those who *have* read it have become creationists!

What can creationists do to help bring about a more equitable treatment of this vital issue in the public schools? How can they help their own children in the meantime? The following suggestions are in order of recommended priority. All involve effort and expense, but the stakes are high and the need is urgent.

1. Most basic is the necessity for each concerned creationist himself to become informed on the issue and the scientific facts involved. He does not need to be a scientist to do this, but merely to read several of the scholarly creationist books that are now available. He should also study creationist literature that demonstrates the fallacious nature of the various compromising positions (e.g., theistic evolution, day-age theory,

gap theory, local flood theory, etc.) in order to be on solid ground in his own convictions.

2. He should then see that his own children and young people, as well as others for whom he is concerned, have access to similar literature on their own level. He also should be aware of the teachings they are currently receiving in school and help them find answers to the problems they are encountering. He should encourage them always to be gracious and respectful to the teacher, but also to look for opportunities (in speeches, term papers, quizzes, etc.) to show that, although they understand the arguments for evolution, the creationist model can also be held and presented scientifically.

3. If he learns of teachers who are obviously bigoted and unfair toward students of creationist convictions, it would be well for him to talk with the teacher himself, as graciously as possible, pointing out the true nature of the issue and requesting the teacher to present both points of view to the students. Under some circumstances, this might be followed up by similar talks with the principal and superintendent.

4. Many teachers and administrators are quite willing to present both viewpoints, but have been unaware that there does exist a solid scientific case for creation, and, therefore, they don't know how to do this. There is thus a great need for teachers, room libraries, and school libraries to be supplied with sound creationist literature. Perhaps some schools, or even districts, will be willing to provide such literature themselves. If not, the other alternative is for parental associations, churches, or individuals to take on such a project as a public service. If sound creationist books are conveniently available, many teachers (not all, unfortunately, but far more than at present) would be willing to use them and to encourage their students to use them.

5. Creationist parents, teachers, pastors, and others can join forces to sponsor meetings, seminars, teaching in-

stitutes, etc., in their localities. Qualified creationist scientists can be invited to speak at such meetings, and if adequate publicity (especially on a person-to-person basis) is given, a real community-wide impact can be made in this way. Especially valuable, when such invitations can be arranged, are opportunities for creationist scientists to speak at meetings of scientists or educators. Also such men can be invited to speak in churches or in other large gatherings of interested laymen.

6. Discussions can be held with officials at high levels (state education boards, district boards, superintendents, etc.) to acquaint them with the evidences supporting creation and the importance of the issue. They can be requested to inform the teachers of their state or district that the equal teaching of evolution and creation, not on a religious basis, but as scientific models, is both permitted and encouraged. Cases of unfair discrimination against creationist minorities in classrooms can be reported, and most officials at such levels are sufficiently concerned with the needs of *all* their constituents that, if they can first be shown there is a valid scientific case for creation and that evolution has at least as much religious character as does creation, they will quite probably favor such a request.

7. Public response can be made (always of a scientific, rather than emotional flavor) to newspaper stories, television programs, etc., which favor evolution. Those responses may be in the form of letters-to-the-editor, protest letters to sponsors, news releases, and other means.

8. Financial support should be provided for those organizations attempting in a systematic way to do scientific research, produce creationist textbooks and other literature, and to provide formal instruction from qualified scientists in the field of creationism. This can be done both through individual gifts and bequests and through budgeted giving by churches and other organizations.

It will be noted that no recommendation is made for political or legal pressure to *force* the teaching of creationism in the schools. Some well-meaning people have tried this, and it may serve the purpose of generating publicity for the creationist movement. In general, however, such pressures are self-defeating. "A man convinced against his will is of the same opinion still."

Force generates reaction, and this is especially true in such a sensitive and vital area as this. The hatchet job accomplished on the fundamentalists by the news media and the educational establishment following the Scopes trial in 1925 is an example of what could happen, in the unlikely event that favorable legislation or court decisions could be obtained by this route.

Reasonable persuasion is the better route. "The servant of the Lord must not strive; but be gentle unto all men, apt to teach, patient, In meekness instructing those that oppose themselves" (II Timothy 2:24,25).

The following is a reprint of a letter sent to the California State Board of Education from a concerned parent and local school board member.

December 7, 1972

California State Board of Education
Gentlemen:

I am writing to you in a threefold capacity: as president of the Board of Education of the Morongo Unified School District, as the minister of a large church, and as the father of two children who are being educated in public schools.

It is my understanding that you will soon be deciding as to whether or not you will maintain a previously defined requirement that creationism, in its scientific framework, be included in state adopted textbooks as a valid alternative to evolutionism.

Having carefully studied this subject over a number of years, I submit the following for your consideration:

1. Evolutionism is ultimately unproveable and is, therefore, theoretical and philosophical in nature.
2. Creationism is also ultimately unproveable and is, therefore, also theoretical and philosophical in nature.
3. Both evolutionism and creationism can be made to fit into a scientific framework or model.
4. A thorough study of the subject will reveal that the scientific framework for creationism is, in every way, as valid as that of evolutionism.
5. Creationism is no more religious in its orientation than is evolutionism. Both are ultimately accepted on the basis of faith and not scientific proof. To imply that creationism is religious and that evolutionism is scientific is, in my opinion, a gross violation of intellectual honesty.
6. To present one viewpoint exclusive of the other is to infer that there is only one possible conclusion; and, therefore, the teaching of evolution becomes doctrinaire. In my numerous contacts, I find that many people highly object to this.
7. The ultimate outcome of the exclusive presentation of theory of evolution:
   a. Forces many parents to finance the teaching of philosophical (religious) views and ideals in direct opposition to their own.
   b. Makes it impossible for the student to make an intelligent and rational choice as to what they will believe. To this extent, it destroys academic freedom.
   c. Leaves the student with a foundation that excludes the possibility of theism and an absolute standard for morals, as well as an absolute point of reference for the individual in the universe, and mandates, on the other hand, belief in such philosophies as humanism, pantheism, and materialism.
8. The issue of whether or not creationism should be presented as a valid alternative to evolutionism has an impact that goes well beyond the science classroom into the areas of civics, social studies, government, philosophy, and history. Its importance ought not to be

ignored.

9. In our school district, we are presently studying supplemental texts to broaden the student's knowledge of the alternatives. This ought not to be necessary as this material should be available within the state approved textbooks; especially when the size of the investment is considered.

It is my personal conviction that the cause of quality education will be served much better by an educational process that fairly presents both viewpoints. (I might add that I feel that this is one way public confidence in education can be greatly enhanced.) I therefore recommend for your consideration that:

1. The State Board of Education maintain the present framework requirement of presenting creationism (in its scientific framework) as a valid alternative to evolutionism in all state-adopted science textbooks.

2. The State Board of Education contact the Creation Research Society, which has a membership of over 500 scientists who support and affirm the creationist viewpoint of origins from a scientific standpoint, and contract their services in revising the presently submitted science textbooks so that they will give a fair presentation of both viewpoints. (I would suggest that it would seem unreasonable to contract the services of those who do not know or appreciate the scientific framework of Creationism to produce a fair representation of it.)

I submit three points for clarification:

1. I do not propose that creationism be presented in religious framework, but in its scientific framework.

2. This letter is wholly unsolicited.

3. I do not propose that everyone must be committed to the creationist viewpoint. I only ask, in the interest of fairness, that each member of the State Board of Education allow a fair and broad-minded presentation of both viewpoints so that the students can decide for themselves.

Sincerely yours,   David Innes

THE CENTER OF THE EARTH
Henry M. Morris, Ph.D.

The earth's surface is approximately 70% covered with water, which part is thus uninhabitable by man. The 30% of the earth occupied by land surfaces is not in one single land mass, but is stretched out in an odd-shaped assortment of continents and islands, all of which are either inhabited or potentially habitable by man.

Three of the seven great continents (Europe, Africa, Asia) are actually joined together, as are two others (North America, South America). During the glacial period, the sea level was lower and a land bridge across the Bering Strait connected Eurasia with the Americas. Australia was possibly connected to Asia by a land bridge across the Malaysian Peninsula and the islands of Indonesia.

The major land areas of the world have probably been connected together until fairly recent times, certainly within the period of man's residence on the earth. By the Biblical chronology, in fact, this situation must have prevailed for some period of time after the great Flood and even until after the dispersion at Babel. The Bible says: "Of them (that is, of the descendants of Noah, after the Flood) was the whole earth overspread" (Genesis 9:19). Also, it says:"From thence (that is, from Babel) did the Lord scatter them abroad upon the face of all the earth" (Genesis 11:9).

It is significant that ancient secular historians, as well as modern archaeological researchers, all agree that the development of civilization began somewhere in the so-called "Bible lands," — not in Europe or America or China or South Africa, but rather somewhere in the region where Asia and Europe and Africa join together, most likely in the Tigris-Euphrates region. The ancient nations of Sumeria, Egypt, Elam, Assyria, and others of comparable antiquity, were all centered around this area.

Similarly the beginnings of written communication, of transportation, of animal domestication, of agriculture, and of most other basic ingredients of structured human economies, are known to focus on this region.

At first, one might be tempted to offer these facts in support of the divine inspiration of the Bible, since the Bible does indicate that civilizations existed before the Flood and that therefore men carried with them aspects of that common civilized knowledge as they gradually spread around the world from Mount Ararat and the city of Babel. These facts do, of course, support the general historical accuracy of the Bible, but the historical fact that civilization began in this region does not in itself demonstrate that the writer of Genesis required divine revelation in order to report that fact correctly. He may simply have been a good historian. The rise of civilization in that region might be attributed to favorable physical and climatological conditions rather than to the Genesis story that Noah's Ark landed in the vicinity.

However, there may be a more subtle correlation between the Bible and geography than this, one which cannot be explained in terms of natural physical factors such as climate and soil fertility.

The argument might go like this: since God intended for man to "fill the earth" after the Flood (Genesis 9:1), and since the ark "rested upon the mountains of Ararat" the very day that God restrained the Flood from further destruction (Genesis 8:1-4, compared with Genesis 7:11), wouldn't it be reasonable to think that God had arranged for the "port of disembarkation" to be located somewhere near the geographical center of the land which man was commanded to fill?

This may not be a necessary inference, but it does seem the most appropriate thing for God to do, since He was at this time acting completely in grace toward Noah and his sons. At any rate, it seems to be worth investigating as a hypothesis.

There are a few Scriptural intimations to this effect, though no definite statement. For example, Ezekiel 38:12 speaks of the people of Israel as those "that dwell in the midst of the land" (King James Version). The latter phrase is better translated as "the navel of the earth." Many Bible commentators have interpreted this verse to mean that the land of Israel is located at the geographical center of the earth's land surfaces.

There are also the various references to "the four corners of the earth," or better "the four quarters of the earth" (Isaiah 11:12; Revelation 7:1; Revelation 20:8). This is the standard terminology for directional identification by which land areas are divided into four quadrants (northeast, northwest, southwest, southeast), with the "origin of coordinates" or "center," from which directions are measured, being placed at the focal point of interest. Invariably, in Scripture, this focal point, to which all directions are oriented, is assumed to be in Israel, or even more specifically, at Jerusalem.

It is significant that these "Bible lands" were not only the center of dispersion of the nations after the Flood when God told those who had been saved to go out and multiply and "fill the earth," but were also the center of dispersion of the news of redemption, when God told those who had been saved to go out into "all the world" with this witness. Once again, the interest of maximum efficiency in the accomplishment of God's work of grace would have been best served, other things being equal, by seeing that this center of evangelistic outreach was established near the earth's geographic center.

Though none of these arguments are fully convincing, we do have the feeling that it would at least somehow be *appropriate* for God to ordain the geography itself to be an expression of His love and concern for man. At least the subject is worth investigating.

As a matter of fact, the location of the earth's geographical center should be a matter of some value entirely apart from any theological considerations. In addition to its purely academic and esthetic interest, there could be innumerable future applications of this information. If ever there is to be a world administration, or a world communications center, or a world center of education or transportation or commerce or almost any organized activity of mankind as a whole, the most efficient location for such systems would logically be near the geographical center of the world's inhabited lands.

Other things being equal, the cost of operating such systems would be minimized and the ease of utilizing such systems would be maximized if their hubs were located reasonably near the center of all the subsystems around the world that would have to be keyed into them. The location of the center of the earth is thus desireable not only esthetically and theologically, but also scientifically and economically.

Until the present time, however, such information could not have been acquired at all. In the first place, the geography of the earth's land areas would have to be mapped with reasonable accuracy, and this was not accomplished until modern times.

However, the geography of the continents and islands is so intricately complex that there was no feasible way of calculating their center until the advent of the high-speed digital computer. If the earth had only one continent, and if it had a regular geometric shape (say a circle or rectangle), it would be easy enough to determine its center. But the actual situation is of course vastly more complicated.

The problem is basically to determine that point on the earth's surface, the average distance from which to all other points on the earth's land surfaces is a minimum. This point is defined as the earth's geographical center.

1. Divide all the earth's land areas into small, equal, unit areas.
2. Select one of these unit areas as a possible location of earth's center.
3. Measure the distance along the earth's surface from this reference area to *each* of the other unit areas, all over the earth.
4. Add up all these distances and divide the total by the number of individual distances measured. The result is the *average distance* from the reference area to all the other unit areas around the world.
5. Repeat the entire process in steps (1) through (4) above for *each one* of all the other unit areas around the world.

6. Compare the "average distances" so calculated for all the different unit areas. The one for which the average distance turns out to be the smallest is the earth's geographical center.

Actually, the calculation becomes feasible only if it can be programmed on a high-speed computer. To accomplish the latter requires a knowledge of spherical trigonometry, geodesy, calculus, and computer science. In addition, there must be available accurate data on the earth's land and water areas, arranged in a grid network tied to latitude and longitude. With these factors present, the computation then becomes quite feasible.

Results

This particular research investigation was first proposed by Andrew J. Woods, M.S., a physicist with Gulf Energy and Environmental Sciences in San Diego. The project was sponsored by the Institute for Creation Research to the extent of providing funds for computer time rental and for publication of the resulting Technical Monograph. Mr. Woods performed all the analyses and programming on his own time. His results are summarized in the form of a project report, incorporated now in that Monograph. The theory behind the analysis, the computer results, and his conclusions are all given in detail there.

The most significant conclusion, of course, is that the geographical center of the earth is indeed located in the so-called "Bible lands," as the Biblical and theological considerations discussed earlier would imply.

This fact is significant statistically. If we consider the Bible lands to be bounded roughly by Memphis (the capital of ancient Egypt) on the south and west (latitude 30°, longitude 31°), and Ararat on the north and east (latitude 39°, longitude 44°), this will include Babylon (latitude 32°, longitude 35°), as well as practically all the cities in which the events narrated in the Old Testament took place. The land area contained in this quadrangle (between latitudes 30° and 39°, and longitudes 31° and 44°), is approximately 440,000 square miles. The total land area of the earth's surface is approximately 197,000,000 square miles, 450 times greater.

Therefore, the probability that the earth's center would happen to fall in these Bible lands is only one chance out of 450. This is highly significant, from a statistical point of view, even more so in light of the Biblical inferences to this effect, and is strong evidence of divine planning. The events could just as well have taken place, so far as chance is concerned, in any one of 449 other land areas of equal size elsewhere, land areas *not* containing the earth's geographical hub.

The *exact* center of the earth, insofar as Mr. Woods' calculations could determine, was found to be near Ankara, the present capital of Turkey, at latitude 39° and longitude 34°, on the same latitude as Mount Ararat and essentially the same longitude as Jerusalem.

Theologically speaking, it might have seemed more appropriate for this exact center to have turned out to be in Jerusalem, or else at Mount Ararat or possibly Babel. Of these three, it is essentially equidistant, about 550 miles, from Ararat and Jerusalem.

However, since there is no explicit statement in the Bible requiring the earth's center to be precisely at Ararat or Babel or Jerusalem, all of the implications of Scripture in this regard are well satisfied if the center is somewhere in these Bible lands. Interestingly, the earth's center at Ankara, together with Jerusalem, Ararat and Babylon form almost a perfect square.

As far as the needs of a potential center of world activities are concerned, these also would be met by a site anywhere in this region. Other factors besides that of precise centrality would of course have to be considered in the choice of such a location.

The calculations made by Woods indicate, in fact, that the average distance to all the world's land areas varies only slightly for any central site in all this general region. For example, the average distance from the Ankara region was found to be 4597 miles, whereas the average distance from the Jerusalem area is 4612 miles and from the Ararat region is 4617 miles, a difference of only 15 miles and 20 miles, respectively, or about ⅓%. In terms of practical applications, the difference is negligible.

By way of contrast, the location of the earth's "anti-center" — that is, the point with the *greatest* average distance to all the earth's land areas, was found to be in the South Pacific, at a point of latitude -45° and longitude -150°. This point is east of the southern tip of New Zealand and west of the southern tip of South America, far from land of any kind. This would be the *worst* place to locate any kind of world activity center! The average distance to the land areas of the earth from this point was found to be 7813 miles.

This article is included as Appendix B in the book *Adventure on Ararat*, available from I.C.R. (March 15, 1973) $1.50, paper. For a full discussion of the above research study, with complete analysis, obtain the I.C.R. Technical Monograph No. 3, *The Center of the Earth*, by Andrew J. Woods, M.S. (published 1973) $1.50.

EVOLUTION, THERMODYNAMICS,
AND ENTROPY

Henry M. Morris, Ph.D.

Definitions

The study of biological processes and phenomena indicates that significant evolutionary developments are not observable in the modern world. Similarly the great gaps in the fossil record make it extremely doubtful that any genuine evolution, as distinct from small changes within the kinds, ever took place in the past.

There is one consideration, however, which goes well beyond the implications of the above difficulties. Not only is there no evidence that evolution ever *has* taken place, but there is also firm evidence that evolution never *could* take place. The *law* of *increasing entropy* is an impenetrable barrier which no evolutionary mechanism yet suggested has ever been able to overcome. Evolution and entropy are opposing and mutually exclusive concepts. If the entropy principle is really a universal law, then evolution must be impossible.

The very terms themselves express contradictory concepts. The word "evolution" is of course derived from a Latin word meaning "out-rolling". The picture is of an outward-progressing spiral, an unrolling from an infinitesimal beginning through ever-broadening circles, until finally all reality is embraced within.

"Entropy", on the other hand, means literally "in-turning". It is derived from the two Greek words *en* (meaning "in") and *trope* (meaning "turning"). The concept is of something spiraling inward upon itself, exactly the opposite concept to "evolution". Evolution is change outward and upward, entropy is change inward and downward.

That the principles of evolution and entropy are both believed to be universal principles and yet are mutually contradictory is seen from the following authoritative definitions:

"There is a general natural tendency of all observed systems to go from order to disorder, reflecting dissipation of energy available for future transformation — the law of increasing entropy."[1]

As far as evolution is concerned, the classic definition of Sir Julian Huxley is as follows:

"Evolution in the extended sense can be defined as a directional and essentially irreversible process occurring in time, which in its course gives rise to an increase of variety and an increasingly high level of organization in its products. Our present knowledge indeed forces us to the view that the whole of reality *is* evolution — a single process of self-transformation."[2]

Thus, in the one instance, "all observed systems . . . go from order to disorder," and in the other, "the whole of reality . . . gives rise to an increasingly high level of organization in its products." It seems obvious that either evolution or entropy has been vastly over-rated or else that something is wrong with the English language.

The entropy principle, however, is nothing less than the Second Law of Thermodynamics, which is as universal and certain a law as exists in science. First, however, before discussing the Second Law, we should define the First Law and, for that matter, thermodynamics itself.

Thermodynamics is a compound of two Greek words, *therme* ("heat") and *dunamis* ("power"). It is the science that treats of the power or energy contained in heat, and its conversion to other forms of energy. The term "energy" is itself derived from the Greek word *energeia* ("working"), and is normally defined as "the capacity to do work." In modern scientific terminology, "energy" and "work" are considered equivalent, each measured as the product of a force times the distance through which it acts (foot-pounds, in the English system of dimensions). Something which has "energy" has the "capacity to do work" . . . that is, the "capacity to exert a force through a distance."

The concept of "power" is closely related to that of "energy", except that the time factor must also be taken into account. Power is the work done, or the energy expended to do the work, per unit of time measured in foot-pounds per second.

The First Law of Thermodynamics

Since all processes are fundamentally energy conversion processes, and since everything that happens in the physical universe is a "process" of some kind, it is obvious why the Two Laws of Thermodynamics are recognized as the most universal and fundamental of all scientific laws. Everything that *exists* in the universe is some form of energy, and everything that *happens* is some form of energy conversion. Thus the Laws which govern energy and energy conversion are of paramount importance in understanding the world we live in.

Isaac Asimov defines the First Law as follows:

"To express all this, we can say: 'Energy can be transferred from one place to another, or transformed from one form to another, but it can be neither created nor destroyed.' Or we can put it another way: 'The total quantity of energy in the universe is constant.' When the total quantity of something does not change, we say that it is conserved. The two statements given above, then, are two ways of expressing 'the law of conservation of energy.' This law is considered the most powerful and most fundamental generalization about the universe that scientists have ever been able to make."[3]

Asimov makes a very interesting point when he says concerning this Law: "No one knows *why* energy is conserved."[4] He should have said, of course, that *science* cannot tell us why energy is neither created nor destroyed. The Bible, however, does give us this information.

The reason why no energy can now be created is because only God can create energy and because God has "rested from all His work which He created and made" (Genesis 2:3). The reason why energy cannot now be destroyed is because He is now "upholding all things by the word of His power" (Hebrews 1:3). "I know that, whatsoever God doeth, it shall be forever: nothing can be put to it, nor anything taken from it" (Ecclesiastes 3:14).

The Second Law in Classical Thermodynamics

The First Law is itself a strong witness against evolution, since it implies a basic condition of stability in the universe. The fundamental structure of the cosmos is one of conservation, not innovation. However, this fact in itself is not impressive to the evolutionist, as he merely assumes that the process of evolution takes place within the framework of energy conservation, never stopping to wonder where all the energy came from in the first place nor how it came to pass that the total energy was constant from then on.

It is the Second Law, however, that wipes out the theory of evolution. There *is* a universal process of change, and it *is* a directional change, but it is *not* an upward change.

In the so-called classical thermodynamics, the Second Law, like the First, is formulated in terms of energy.

"It is in the transformation process that Nature appears to exact a penalty and this is where the second principle makes its appearance. For every naturally occurring transformation of energy is accompanied, somewhere, by a loss in the *availability* of energy for the future performance of work."[5]

In this case, entropy can be expressed mathematically in terms of the total irreversible flow of heat. It expresses quantitatively the amount of energy in an energy conversion process which becomes unavailable for further work. In order for work to be done, the available energy has to "flow" from a higher level to a lower level. When it reaches the lower level, the energy is still in existence, but no longer capable of doing work. Heat will naturally flow from a hot body to a cold body, but not from a cold body to a hot body.

For this reason, no process can be 100% efficient, with all of the available energy converted into work. Some must be deployed to overcome friction and will be degraded to non-recoverable heat energy, which will finally be radiated into space and dispersed. For the same reason a self-contained perpetual motion machine is an impossibility.

Since, as we have noted, everything in the physical universe is energy in some form and, since in every process some energy becomes unavailable, it is obvious that ultimately *all* energy in the universe will be unavailable energy, if present processes go on long enough. When that happens, presumably all the various forms of energy in the universe will have been gradually converted through a multiplicity of processes into uniformly (that is, randomly) dispersed heat energy. Everything will be at the same low temperature. There will be no "differential" of energy levels, therefore no "gradient" of energy to induce its flow. No more work can be done and the universe will reach what the physicists call its ultimate "heat death."

Thus, the Second Law proves, *as certainly as science can prove anything whatever*, that the universe had a beginning. Similarly, the First Law shows that the universe could not have begun itself. The total quantity of energy in the universe is a constant, but the quantity of *available* energy is decreasing. Therefore, as we go *backward* in time, the available energy would have been progressively greater until, finally, we would reach the beginning point, where available energy equalled total energy. Time could go back no further than this. At this point both energy and time must have come into existence. Since energy could not create itself, the most scientific and logical conclusion to which we could possibly come is that: "In the beginning, God created the heaven and the earth."

The evolutionist will not accept this conclusion, however, He hypothesizes that either: (1) some natural law cancelling out the Second Law prevailed far back in time, or (2) some natural law cancelling out the Second Law prevails far out in space.

When he makes such assumptions, however, he is denying his own theory, which says that all things can be explained in terms of presently observable laws and processes. He is really resorting to creationism, but refuses to acknowledge a Creator.

Entropy and Disorder

A second way of stating the entropy law is in terms of statistical thermodynamics. It is recognized today that not only are all scientific laws empirical but also that they are statistical. A great number of individual molecules, in a gas for example, may behave in such a way that the over-all aspects of that gas produce predictable patterns in the aggregate, even though individual molecules may deviate from the norm. Laws describing such behavior must be formulated statistically, or probabilistically, rather than strictly dynamically. The dynamical laws then can theoretically be deduced as limiting cases of the probabilistic statements.

In this context, entropy is a probability function related to the degree of disorder in a system. The more disordered a system may be, the more likely it is.

"All real processes go with an increase of entropy. The entropy also measures the randomness, or lack of orderliness of the system; the greater the randomness, the greater the entropy."[6]

Note again the universality expressed here *all real processes*. Isaac Asimov expresses this concept interestingly as follows:

"Another way of stating the Second Law then is: 'The universe is constantly getting more disorderly!' Viewed that way, we can see the Second Law all about us. We have to work hard to straighten a room but left to itself it becomes a mess again very quickly and very easily. Even if we never enter it, it becomes dusty and musty. How difficult to maintain houses, and machinery, and our own bodies in perfect working order; how easy to let them deteriorate. In fact, all we have to do is nothing, and everything deteriorates, collapses, breaks down, wears out, all by itself and that is what the Second Law is all about."[7]

Remember this tendency from order to disorder applies to all real processes. Real processes include, of course, biological and geological processes, as well as chemical and physical processes. The interesting question is: "How does a real biological process, which goes from order to disorder, result in evolution, which goes from disorder to order?" Perhaps the evolutionist can ultimately find an answer to this question, but he at least should not ignore it, as most evolutionists do.

Especially is such a question vital, when we are thinking of evolution as a growth process on the grand scale from atom to Adam and from particle to people. This represents an absolutely *gigantic* increase in order and complexity, and is clearly out of place together in the context of the Second Law.

References

1. R. B. Lindsay: "Physics — To What Extent Is It Deterministic?" *American Scientist*, Vol. 56, Summer 1968, p. 100.
2. Julian Huxley: "Evolution and Genetics" in *What is Man?* (Ed. by J. R. Newman, New York, Simon and Schuster, 1955), p. 278.
3. Isaac Asimov: "In the Game of Energy and Thermodynamics You Can't Break Even," *Smithsonian Institute Journal*, June, 1970, p.6.
4. *Ibid.*
5. R. B. Lindsay: "Entropy Consumption and Values in Physical Science," *American Scientist*, Vol. 47, September, 1959, p. 378.
6. Harold Blum: "Perspectives in Evolution," *American Scientist*, October, 1955, p. 595.
7. Isaac Asimov: *op cit*, p. 10.

CREATION-EVOLUTION

Duane T. Gish, Ph.D.

There is the theory that all living things have arisen through a naturalistic, mechanistic evolutionary process from a single source, which itself arose by a similar process from a dead, inorganic world. This general evolutionary hypothesis is usually presented as an established scientific fact in science textbooks. All of the evidence that can be adduced in favor of this theory is thoroughly discussed in such texts, and it is often stated that all competent biologists accept the theory of evolution.

While it is true that most biologists accept evolution as a fact, there is a significant minority of competent biologists who do not accept this theory as the best interpretation of the known data. One of these who may be cited as an example is Dr. W. R. Thompson (see American Men of Science or Canadian Men of Science), whose credentials as a competent biologist need no defense. His objections to evolutionary theory may be found in his introduction to a 1956 edition of Charles Darwin's *Origin of Species* entitled *A Critique of Evolution* (1). In 1963 a group of scientists formed the Creation Research Society (2). This relatively new organization now includes about 400 members, all of whom hold a master's degree or doctorate in some field of science. None accepts the theory of evolution.

There is actually a considerable body of sound, scientific evidence that contradicts the theory of evolution, some of which appears to be absolutely incompatible with the theory. The importance of the nature of this evidence is never emphasized in textbooks used in our public school systems and colleges. In fact, this evidence is rarely, if ever, even mentioned. As a result, biology students are exposed to all the evidence that can be adduced in favor of the theory, but are not made aware of its weaknesses, nor the evidence that actually contradicts the theory. We must recognize, therefore, that such an educational process amounts to indoctrination in a particular world-view or philosophy based on the concept that the origin of the universe, the origin and diversity of life, in fact all of reality, must be explainable solely on the basis of the laws of chemistry and physics. The possibility of a Creator or the existence of a Supernatural Being is excluded. We are convinced that the reason evolutionary theory is so widely accepted today is because our scientists and biology teachers are the products of an educational system dominated by this naturalistic, mechanistic, humanistic philosophy.

The theory of evolution violates two of the most fundamental laws of nature — the First and Second Laws of Thermodynamics. The First Law states that no matter what changes may take place, nuclear, chemical, or physical, the sum total of energy and matter (actually equivalent) remains constant. Nothing now is being either created nor destroyed, although transformations of many kinds may take place. The Second Law states that every change which takes place naturally and spontaneously tends to go from a state of order to one of disorder, from the complex to the simple, from a higher energy state to a lower energy state. The total amount of randomness or disorder in the universe (entropy is a measure of this randomness) is constantly and inevitably increasing. Any increase in order and complexity that may occur, therefore, could only be local and temporary; but evolution requires a general increase in order extending through geological time. Amino acids do not spontaneously combine to form proteins, but proteins spontaneously break down to amino acids, and amino acids slowly break down to simpler chemical compounds. With careful control of reactants, energy input, and removal of product from the energy source (as is done in current "origin of life" experiments), man can synthesize amino acids from gases, and proteins from amino acids. But under any combination of realistic primordial earth conditions, these processes could never have taken place. This fact was adequately demonstrated by Hull who concluded that, "The physical chemist, guided by the proved principles of chemical thermodynamics and kinetics, cannot offer any encouragement to the biochemist, who needs an ocean full of organic compounds to form even lifeless coacervates" (3). Hull was here referring to origin of life speculations.

Since the universe, like a clock, is running down, it is obvious that it hasn't existed forever. But according to the First Law, the sum total of energy and matter is always a constant. How then can we, purely on a natural basis alone, explain the origin of matter and energy of which this universe is composed. The evolutionary continuum, from cosmos to man, is creative and progressive, while the First and Second Laws of Thermodynamics declare that known natural processes are quantitatively degenerative. In every case, without exception, when these Laws have been subjected to test they have been found valid. Exponents of evolutionary theory thus ignore the observable in order to accept the unobservable (the evolutionary origin of life and of the major kinds of living things).

The evolutionary process has supposedly taken place via random mutational changes. This basic concept of the modern evolutionary theory is under attack even by some evolutionists. Salisbury (4) has recently questioned this concept and it has come under attack by several mathematicians. A symposium was held at the Wistar Institute in 1966 at which these mathematicians and evolutionary biologists presented opposing views (5). One of the mathematicians, Dr. Murray Eden, stated that, "It is our contention that if 'random' is given a serious and crucial interpretation from a probabilistic point of view, the randomness postulate is highly implausible and that an *adequate scientific theory of evolution must await the discovery of new natural laws — physical, physicochemical and biological*" (emphasis added) (6). It is the contention of Salisbury and of these mathematicians that the increase in complexity and the progress that has supposedly been accomplished by evolution through *random* changes would require a length of time billions of times longer than three billion years.

Random mutations and natural selection supposedly have been responsible for evolution, allegedly a creative and progressive process. Natural selection, however, is not creative since it cannot create anything new. It is a conservative force eliminating the unfit. Random mutational change in an ordered system is a disordering or randomizing process and is thus degenerative, not progressive. This realization is slowly spreading among evolutionists today.

Whether evolution actually did happen or not can only be indicated by an examination of the historical record, that is, the fossil record. What type of evidence would support the evolutionary concept? Thompson has stated, "Therefore, if we found in the geological strata a series of fossils showing a gradual transition from simple to complex forms, and could be sure that they correspond to a true time-sequence, then we should be inclined to feel that Darwinian evolution has occurred, even though its mechanism remains unknown" (1). If invertebrate gave rise to vertebrate, fish to amphibia, amphibian to reptile, reptile to bird and mammal — each transformation requiring millions of years and involving innumerable transitional forms — then the fossil record should certainly produce a good representative number of these transitional types. Thompson goes on to say, "That is certainly what Darwin would have liked to report, but of course he was unable to do so. What the available data indicated was a remarkable absence of the many intermediate forms required by the theory; the absence of the primitive types that should have existed in the strata regarded as the most ancient; and the sudden appearance of the principle taxonomic groups." Later on he states, ". . . and I may note that the position is not notably different today. The modern Darwinian paleontologists are obliged, just like their predecessors and like Darwin, to water down the facts with subsidiary hypotheses which however plausible are in the nature of things unverifiable."

In the Cambrian geological strata there occurs a sudden, great outburst of fossils of animals on a highly developed level of complexity. In the Cambrian rocks are found billions of fossils of animals so complex that the evolutionists estimate they would have required one and a half billion years to evolve. Trilobites, brachiopods, sponges, corals, jellyfish, in fact every one of the major invertebrate forms of life are found in the Cambrian. What is found in rocks supposedly older than the Cambrian, that is in the so-called pre-Cambrian rocks? Not a single indisputable fossil! Certainly it can be said without fear of contradiction, the evolutionary predecessors of the Cambrian fauna have never been found.

Axelrod, a geologist and an evolutionist, has written: "One of the major unsolved problems of geology and evolution is the occurrence of diversified, multi-cellular marine invertebrates in Lower Cambrian rocks and their absence in rocks of greater age. These Early Cambrian fossils included porifera, coelenterates, brachiopods, mollusca, echinoids, and arthropods. Their high degree of organization clearly indicates that a long period of evolution preceded their appearance in the record. However, when we turn to examine the pre-Cambrian rocks for the forerunners of these Early Cambrian fossils, *they are nowhere to be found.* Many thick (over 5000 feet) sections of sedimentary rock are now known to lie in unbroken succession below strata containing the earliest Cambrian fossils. These sediments apparently were suitable for the preservation of fossils because they are often identical with overlying rocks which are fossiliferous, *yet no fossils are found in them*" (emphasis added) (7).

George Gaylord Simpson, famous paleontologist and evolutionist, has termed the absence of pre-Cambrian fossils the "major mystery of the history of life" (8). This great outburst of highly developed and complex living things is highly contradictory to evolutionary theory, but is exactly what would be predicted on the basis of special (divine) creation.

The fossil record ought to produce thousands of transitional forms. Instead we find that there is a regular and systematic absence of transitional forms between higher categories. The major invertebrate types found in the Cambrian are just as distinctly set apart when they first appear as they are today, the fossil record giving no indication that any of these major types have been derived from common ancestors.

The vertebrates supposedly evolved from an invertebrate. This is an assumption that cannot be documented from the fossil record. There is a vast gulf between the invertebrates and vertebrates not bridged by transitional forms. The first vertebrate, a fish of the class Agnatha, is a 100% vertebrate. Of its possible evolutionary origin, Ommanney has said, "How this earliest chordate stock evolved, what stages of development it went through to eventually give rise to truly fishlike creatures we do not know. Between the Cambrian when it probably originated and the Ordovician when the first fossils of animals with really fishlike characteristics appeared, there is a gap of perhaps 100 million years which we will probably never be able to fill" (9). One hundred million years and no transitional forms! Incredible!

Fish supposedly gave rise to amphibian over a period of millions of years during which time the fins of the hypothetical ancestral fish gradually changed into the feet and legs of the amphibian. Yet not a single fossil has ever been found showing a part-way fin and part-way foot! The living amphibians include three types: the salamanders and newts, usually with sprawling legs and tails; the frogs and toads, among the most highly specialized of all land vertebrates, having no tails and very long hind legs; the Apodans, a worm-like creature with no trace of limbs. No transitional forms can be found between these diverse living amphibians, or between them and fossil amphibians (10).

Birds are alleged to have evolved from the reptiles. Yet no one has ever found a single fossil showing a part-way wing and part-way forelimb, or a part-way feather.

135

Archaeopteryx, "the oldest known bird," had teeth but so did other birds found in the fossil record that were unquestionably 100% birds. *Archaeopteryx* had claw-like appendages on the leading edges of its wings. These same appendages, however, are found in a living bird in South America, the *Hoactzin*, and he is 100% bird. *Archeaopteryx* had vertebrae extending out along the tail, but was no more a transitional form between reptile and bird than the bat is a link between bird and mammal. *Archaeopteryx* had fully developed wings and feathers. It flew. It was definitely a bird, as all paleontologists agree. Lecomte du Nouy, an evolutionist, has said, "In spite of the fact that it is undeniably related to the two classes of reptiles and birds (a relation which the anatomy and physiology of actually living specimens demonstrates), we are not even authorized to consider the exceptional case of the *Archaeopteryx* as a true link. By link, we mean a necessary stage of transition between classes such as reptiles and birds, or between smaller groups. An animal displaying characters belonging to two different groups cannot be treated as a true link as long as the intermediary stages have not been found, and as long as the mechanisms of transition remain unknown" (11). Marshall has stated, "The origin of birds is largely a matter of deduction. There is no fossil of the stages through which the remarkable change from reptile to bird was achieved" (12).

As a matter of fact, the ability to fly supposedly evolved four times independently: in the birds, the flying reptiles (pterosaurs) now extinct, the insects, and in mammals (the bat). In *none* of these cases are there fossil transitional forms showing the ability to fly as evolving. Dr. E. C. Olson, an evolutionary geologist, has said, "As far as flight is concerned there are some very big gaps in the records" (13). Concerning insects Olson says, "There is almost nothing to give any information about the history of the origin of flight in insects." Referring to pterosaurs Olson states ". . . there is absolutely no sign of intermediate stages." After referring to *Archaeopteryx* as reptile-like Olson says, "It shows itself to be a bird." Finally, with reference to mammals Olson states, "The first evidence of flight in mammals is in fully developed bats of the Eocene epoch." We thus have a most remarkable situation. Four times a marvelous transformation has taken place: terrestrial animals have evolved the power of flight. Each such transformation required millions of years and involved thousands of transitional forms. Yet none of these transitional forms can be found in the fossil record! Could it be that these transitional forms are not found simply because they never existed? Such evidence can be much more easily correlated within a creationist framework than within an evolutionary framework.

The examples given above are not exceptions, but as stated earlier the fossil record displays a systematic absence of transitional types between higher categories. Even with reference to the famous horse "series," du Nouy reports, "But each one of these intermediaries seems to have appeared 'suddenly,' and it has not yet been possible, because of the lack of fossils, to reconstitute the passage between these intermediaries . . The continuity we surmise may never be established by facts" (14).

We believe that the sudden appearance in the fossil record of highly developed forms of life in vast numbers and the sudden appearance of each major taxonomic group without apparent transitional forms indicates that there was actually no passage at all from lower forms to higher forms, but that each major taxonomic group was specially created and thus corresponds to the "kinds" described in the Book of Genesis.

Professor G. A. Kerkut, an evolutionist, in his illuminating book *Implications of Evolution* has stated ". . there is the theory that all living forms in the world have arisen from a single source which itself came from an inorganic form. (15). This theory can be called the 'General Theory of Evolution' *and the evidence that supports it is not sufficiently strong to allow us to*

137

consider it as anything more than a working hypothesis" (emphasis added). We believe that special creation actually offers a far better explanation of the scientific evidence. To restrict the teaching concerning origins to a single theory, that of organic evolution, and to teach it as an established scientific fact, constitutes indoctrination in a humanistic religious philosophy. Such a procedure violates the Constitutional prohibition against the teaching of sectarian religious views just as clearly as if the teaching concerning origins were restricted to the Book of Genesis. In the spirit of fairness and of academic freedom we plead for a balanced presentation of all the evidence.

References

1. W. R. Thompson; *Critique of Evolution*, an introduction to *Origin of Species*, Charles Darwin; E. P. Dutton and Co., New York, 1956.
2. 2717 Cranbrook Road, Ann Arbor, Michigan 48104.
3. D. E. Hull; *Nature*, *186*, 693 (1960).
4. F. B. Salisbury; *The American Biology Teacher*, *33*, 335 (1971).
5. P. S. Moorehead and M. M. Kaplan, Eds.; *Mathematical Challenges to the Neo-Darwinian Interpretation of Evolution;* Wistar Institute Press, Philadelphia, Penn. 1967.
6. M. Eden;ref. 5, p. 109.
7. D. I. Axelrod; *Science*, *128*, 7 (1958).
8. G. G. Simpson; *The Meaning of Evolution;* Yale University Press, New Haven, 1953, p. 18.
9. F. D. Ommanney, *The Fishes;* Life Nature Library, 1964; p. 60.
10. A. S. Romer; *Vertebrate Paleontology*, 3rd Ed.; University of Chicago Press, Chicago 1966; p. 98.
11. L. du Nouy; *Human Destiny;* The New American Library of World Literature, Inc.; New York, 1947, p. 58.
12. A. J. Marshall, Ed.; *Biology and Comparative Physiology of Birds;* Academic Press, New York, 1960, p. 1.

13. E. C. Olson; *The Evolution of Life;* The New American Library, New York, 1966; p. 180.
14. L. du Nouy; Ref. 11, p. 74.
15. G. A. Kerkut; *Implications of Evolution;* Pergamon Press, New York, 1960, p. 157.

EVOLUTION
AND THE BIBLE
Henry M. Morris, Ph.D.

The evolutionary system has been entrenched for so long that many people who otherwise accept the Bible as infallible have deemed it expedient to compromise on this issue. Thus, evolution has been called, "God's method of creation"; and the Genesis record of the six days of creation has been reinterpreted in terms of the evolutionary ages of historical geology. These geological ages themselves have been accommodated in Genesis either by placing them in an assumed "gap" between Genesis 1:1 and 1:2 or by changing the "days" of creation into the "ages" of evolution.

Theories of this kind raise more problems than they solve, however. It is more productive to take the Bible literally and then to interpret the actual facts of science within its revelatory framework. If the Bible cannot be understood, it is useless as *revelation*. If it contains scientific fallacies, it could not have been given by *inspiration*.

The specific purpose of this study is to show that all such theories which seek to accommodate the Bible to evolutionary geology are invalid and, therefore, should be abandoned.

Theistic Evolution

Evolution is believed by its leading advocates to be a basic principle of continual development, of increasing order and complexity, throughout the universe. The complex elements are said to have developed from simpler elements, living organisms to have evolved from non-living chemicals, complex forms of life from simpler organisms, and even man himself to have gradually evolved from some kind of ape-like ancestor. Religions, cultures, and other social institutions are likewise believed to be continually evolving into higher forms.

Thus, evolution is a complete world-view, an explanation of origins and meanings without the necessity of a personal God who created and upholds all things. Since this philosophy is so widely and persuasively taught in our schools, Christians are often tempted to accept the compromise position of "theistic evolution", according to which evolution is viewed as God's method of creation. However, this is basically an inconsistent and contradictory position. A few of its fallacies are as follows:

1. It contradicts the Bible record of creation. Ten times in the first chapter of Genesis, it is said that God created plants and animals to reproduce "after their kinds". The Biblical "kind" may be broader than our modern "species" concept, but at least it implies definite limits to variation. The New Testament writers accepted the full historicity of the Genesis account of creation. Even Christ Himself quoted from it as historically accurate and authoritative (Matthew 19:4-6).

2. It is inconsistent with God's methods. The standard concept of evolution involves the development of innumerable misfits and extinctions, useless and even harmful organisms. If this is God's "method of creation", it is strange that He would use such cruel, haphazard, inefficient, wasteful processes. Furthermore, the idea of the "survival of the fittest", whereby the stronger animals eliminate the weaker in the "struggle for existence" is the essence of Darwin's theory of evolution by natural selection, and this whole scheme is flatly contradicted by the Biblical doctrine of love, of unselfish sacrifice, and of Christian charity. The God of the Bible is a God or order and of grace, not a God of confusion and cruelty.

3. The evolutionary philosophy is the intellectual basis of all anti-theistic systems. It served Hitler as the rationale for Nazism and Marx as the supposed scientific basis for communism. It is the basis of the various modern methods of psychology and sociology that treat man merely as a higher animal and which have led to the mis-named "new morality" and ethical relativism. It has provided the pseudo-scientific rationale for racism and military agression. Its whole effect on the world and mankind has been harmful and degrading. Jesus said: "A good tree cannot bring forth evil

fruit" (Matthew 7:18). The evil fruit of the evolutionary philosophy is evidence enough of its evil roots.

Thus, evolution is Biblically unsound, theologically contradictory, and sociologically harmful.

Progressive Creation

Some Christians use the term "progressive creation" instead of "theistic evolution", the difference being the suggestion that God interjected occasional acts of creation at critical points throughout the geological ages. Thus, for example, man's *soul* was created, though his body evolved from an ape-like ancestor.

This concept is less acceptable than theistic evolution, however. It not only charges God with waste and cruelty (through its commitment to the geologic ages) but also with ignorance and impotence. God's postulated intermittent creative efforts show either that He didn't know what He wanted when He started the process or else that He couldn't provide it with enough energy to sustain it until it reached its goal. A god who would have to create man by any such cut-and-try-, discontinuous, injurious method as this can hardly be the omniscient, omnipotent, loving God of the Bible.

The Day-Age Theory

According to the established system of historical geology, the history of the earth is divided into a number of geological ages. The earth is supposed to have evolved into its present form and inhabitants over a vast span of geologic ages, beginning about five billion years ago.

In contrast, the Biblical revelation tells us that God created the entire universe in six days only a few thousand years ago. Consequently, many Christian scholars have tried to find some way of reinterpreting Genesis to fit the framework of earth history prescribed by the geologists.

The most popular of these devices has been the "day-age" theory, by which the "days" of creation were interpreted figuratively as the "ages" of geology. However, there are many serious difficulties with this theory.

The Hebrew word for "day" is "yom", and this word can occasionally be used to mean an indefinite period of time, if the context warrants. In the overwhelming preponderance of its occurrences in the Old Testament, however, it means a literal day — that is, either an entire solar day or the daylight portion of a solar day. It was, in fact, defined by God Himself the very first time it was used, in Genesis 1:5, where we are told that "God called the light, day." It thus means, in the context, the "day" in the succession of "day and night" or "light and darkness".

Furthermore, the word is never used to mean a definite period of time, in a succession of similar periods (that is, "the first day", "the second day", etc.) or with definite terminal points (that is, as noted by "evening and morning", etc.) unless that period is a literal solar day. And there are hundreds of instances of this sort in the Bible.

Still further, the plural form of the word (Hebrew "yamim") is used over 700 times in the Old Testament and always, without exception, refers to literal "days". A statement in the Ten Commandments, written on a tablet of stone directly by God Himself, is very significant in this connection, where He uses this word and says plainly: "In six days, the Lord made heaven and earth, the sea, and all that in them is" (Exodus 20:11).

Not only is the day-age theory unacceptable Scripturally, but it also is grossly in conflict with the geological position with which it attempts to compromise. There are more than 20 serious contradictions between the Biblical order and events of the creative days and the standard geologic history of the earth and its development, even if it were permissible to interpret the "days" as "ages". For example, the Bible teaches that the earth existed before the stars, that it was initially covered by water, that fruit trees appeared before fishes, that plant life preceded the sun, that the first animals created were the whales, that birds were made before insects, that man was made before woman, and many other such things, all of which are explicitly contradicted by historical geologists and paleontologists.

But the most serious fallacy in the day-age theory is theological. It charges God with the direct responsibility for five billion years of history of purposeless variation, accidental changes, evolutionary blind alleys, numerous misfits and extinctions, a cruel struggle for existence, with preservation of the strong and extermination of the weak, of natural disasters of all kinds, rampant disease, disorder, and decay, and, above all, with death. The Bible teaches that, at the end of the creation period, God pronounced His whole creation to be "very good", in spite of all this. It also teaches plainly that this present type of world, "groaning and travailing in pain" (Romans 8:22) only resulted from man's sin and God's curse thereon. "By one man sin entered into the world, and death by sin" (Romans 5:12). "God is not the author of confusion" (I Corinthians 14:33).

The Gap Theory

Two theories for harmonizing the first chapter of Genesis with the geologic ages have been advanced, one placing the geologic ages "during" the six days of creation (thus making the "days" into "ages"), and the other placing the geologic ages "before" the six days (thus making them days of "recreation" following a great cataclysm which had destroyed the primeval earth). The "day-age theory" has been shown to be an impossible compromise, both Biblically and scientifically.

The "gap theory" likewise involves numerous serious fallacies. The geologic ages cannot be disposed of merely by ignoring the extensive fossil record on which they are based. These supposed ages are inextricably involved in the entire structure of the evolutionary history of the earth and its inhabitants, up to and including man. The fossil record is the best evidence for evolution (in fact, the only such evidence which indicates evolution on more than a trivial scale). Furthermore, the geologic ages are recognized and identified specifically by the fossil contents of the sedimentary rocks in the earth's crust. The very names of the ages show this. Thus, the "Paleozoic Era" is the era of "ancient life", the "Mesozoic Era" of "intermediate life", and the "Cenozoic Era" of "recent life". As a matter of fact, the one primary means for dating these rocks in the first place has always been the supposed "stage-of-evolution" of the contained fossils.

Thus, acceptance of the geologic ages implicitly involves acceptance of the whole evolutionary package. Most of the fossil forms preserved in the sedimentary rocks have obvious relatives in the present world, so that the "re-creation" concept involves the Creator in "re-creating" in six days many of the same animals and plants which had been previously developed slowly over long ages, only to perish violently in a great pre-Adamic cataclysm.

The gap theory, therefore, really does not face the evolution issue at all, but merely pigeon-holes it in an imaginary gap between Genesis 1:1 and 1:2. It leaves unanswered the serious problem as to why God would use the method of slow evolution over long ages in the primeval world, then destroy it, and then use the method of special creation to re-create the same forms He had just destroyed.

Furthermore, there is no geologic evidence of such a worldwide cataclysm in recent geologic history. In fact, the very concept of a worldwide cataclysm precludes the geologic ages, which are based specifically on the assumption that there have been *no* such worldwide cataclysms. As a device for harmonizing Genesis with geology, the gap theory is self-defeating.

The greatest problem with the theory is, again, that it makes God the direct author of evil. It implies that He used the methods of struggle, violence, decay, and death on a worldwide scale for at least three billion years in order to accomplish His unknown purposes in the primeval world. This is the testimony of the fossils and

145

the geologic ages which the theory tries to place before Genesis 1:2. Then, according to the theory, Satan sinned against God in heaven (Isaiah 14:12-15; Ezekiel 28:11-17), and God cast him out of heaven to the earth, destroying the earth in the process in the supposed pre-Adamic cataclysm. Satan's sin in heaven, however, cannot in any way account for the age-long spectacle of suffering and death in the world during the geologic ages which *preceded* his sin! Thus, God alone remains responsible for suffering, death, and confusion, and without any reason for it.

The Scripture says, on the other hand, at the end of the six days of creation, "And God saw everything that he had made (e.g., including not only the entire earth and all its contents, but all the heavens as well — note Genesis 1:16; 2:2, etc.) and, behold, it was very good" (Genesis 1:31). Death did not "enter the world" until man sinned (Romans 5:12; I Corinthians 15:21). Evidently even Satan's rebellion in heaven had not yet taken place, because everything was pronounced "very good" there, too.

The real answer to the meaning of the great terrestrial graveyard — the fossil contents of the great beds of hardened sediments all over the world — will be found neither in the slow operation of uniform natural processes over vast ages of time nor in an *imaginary* cataclysm that took place before the six days of God's perfect creation. Rather, it will be found in a careful study of the very *real* worldwide cataclysm described in Genesis 6 through 9 and confirmed in many other parts of the Bible and in the early records of nations and tribes all over the world, namely, the great Flood of the days of Noah. Evidences for and results of this worldwide Flood are discussed in detail in Impact Series No. 6.

Conclusion

Only a few of the many difficulties with the various accommodationist theories have been discussed, but even these have shown that it is impossible to devise a legitimate means of harmonizing the Bible with evolution.

We must conclude, therefore, that if the Bible is really the Word of God (as its writers allege and as we believe) then evolution and its geological age-system must be completely false. Since the Bible cannot be reinterpreted to correlate with evolution, Christians must diligently proceed to correlate the *facts* of science with the Bible.

GEOLOGY AND THE FLOOD
Henry M. Morris, Ph.D.

In the early days of geology, especially during the 17th and 18th centuries, the dominant explanation for the sedimentary rocks and their fossilized contents was that they had been laid down in the great Flood of the days of Noah. This was the view of Steno, the "father of stratigraphy", whose principles of stratigraphic interpretation are still followed today, and of John Woodward, Sir Isaac Newton's hand-picked successor at Cambridge, whose studies on sedimentary processes laid the foundation for modern sedimentology and geomorphology. These men and the other Flood geologists of their day were careful scientists, thoroughly acquainted with the sedimentary rocks and the geophysical processes which formed them. In common with most other scientists of their day, they believed in God and the divine authority of the Bible. Evolution and related naturalistic speculations had been confined largely to the writings of social philosophers and rationalistic theologians.

Toward the end of the 18th century, and especially in the first half of the 19th century, the ancient pagan evolutionary philosophies began to be revived and promoted by the various socialistic revolutionary movements of the times. These could make little headway, however, as long as the scientists were predominantly creationists. Evolution obviously required aeons of geologic time and the scientific community, including the great Isaac Newton himself, was committed to the Usher chronology, with its recent special creation and worldwide Flood.

Therefore, it was necessary, first of all, that the Flood be displaced as the framework of geologic interpretation, so that earth history could once again, as in the days of the ancient Greek and Oriental philosophers, be expanded into great reaches and cycles of time over endless ages. Geologic *catastrophism* must be, at all costs replaced by *uniformitarianism*, which would emphasize the slow uniform processes of the present as a sufficient explanation for all earth structures and past history. This was accomplished in two stages: first, the single cataclysm of the Flood was replaced by the multiple catastrophes and new creations of Cuvier and Buckland, each separated from the next by a long period of uniform processes; second, these periodic catastrophes were gradually de-emphasized and the uniformitarian intervals enlarged until the latter finally incorporated the entire history.

It is significant that this uniformitarian revolution was led, not by professional scientific geologists, but by amateurs, men such as Buckland (a theologian), Cuvier (an anatomist), Buffon (a lawyer), Hutton (an agriculturalist), Smith (a surveyor), Chambers (a journalist), Lyell (a lawyer), and others of similar variegated backgrounds. The acceptance of Lyell's uniformitarianism laid the foundation for the sudden success of Darwinism in the decade following the publication of Darwin's *Origin of Species* in 1859. Darwin frequently acknowledged his debt to Lyell, who he said gave him the necessary time required for natural selection to produce meaningful evolutionary results.

Nevertheless, the actual facts of geology still favored catastrophism, and Flood geology never died completely. Although the uniformitarian philosophers could point to certain difficulties in the Biblical geology of their predecessors, there were still greater difficulties in uniformitarianism. Once uniformitarianism had served its purpose — namely, that of selling the scientific community and the general public on the great age of the earth — then geologists could again use local catastrophic processes whenever required for specific geologic interpretations. Stephen Gould has expressed it this way:

"Methodological uniformitarianism was useful only when science was debating the status of the supernatural in its realm."[1]

Heylmun goes even further:

"The fact is, the doctrine of uniformitarianism is no more 'proved' than some of the early ideas of worldwide cataclysms have been disproved."[2]

With adequate time apparently available, assisted by man's natural inclination to escape from God if possible, Darwin's theory of evolution by chance variation and natural selection was eagerly accepted by the learned world. Pockets of scientific resistance in the religious community were quickly neutralized by key clerical endorsements of the "day-age theory", which seemingly permitted Christians to hang on to Genesis while at the same time riding the popular wave of long ages and evolutionary progress. For those fundamentalists who insisted that the creation week required a literal interpretation, the "gap theory" ostensibly permitted them to do so merely by inserting the geologic ages in an imaginary gap between Genesis 1:1 and 1:2, thus ignoring their evolutionary implications.

The Biblical Deluge was similarly shorn of scientific significance by reinterpreting it in terms of a "Local Flood" or, for those few people who insisted that the Genesis narrative required a universal inundation, a "Tranquil Flood". Lyell himself proposed a worldwide tranquil flood that left no geological traces. In any case, the field of earth history was taken over almost completely by evolutionists.

In turn, this capitulation of the scientists to evolution was an enormous boon to the social revolutionaries, who could now proclaim widely that their theories of social change were grounded in natural science. For example, Karl Marx and the Communists quickly aligned themselves with evolutionary geology and biology, Marx even asking to dedicate his *Das Kapital* to Charles Darwin.

"However harshly a philosopher may judge this characterization of Marx's theory (i.e., that Marxism unites science and revolution intrinsically and inseparably) an historian can hardly fail to agree that Marx's claim to give scientific guidance to those who would transform society has been one of the chief reasons for his doctrine's enormous influence."[3]

The "science" referred to in the above is, in context, nothing but naturalistic evolution based on uniformitarian

geology. Similarly, Nietzschean racism, Freudian amor-
alism, and military imperialism all had their roots in the
same soil and grew in the same climate.

Yet all the while the foundation was nothing but sand.
Uniformitarian geology was contrary to both the Bible and
to observable science. Now, a hundred years later, the
humanistic and naturalistic culture erected upon that
foundation is beginning to crumble, and men are
beginning again to look critically at the foundation.

The two Biblical compromise positions are now widely
recognized as unacceptable, either theologically or
scientifically. A brief discussion of the fallacies of the
"day-age" and "gap" theories, as well as "theistic
evolution" and "progressive creation" appeared in Impact
Article No. 5 of the *I.C.R. Acts & Facts*, "Evolution and
the Bible".

The local-flood theory is even less defensible. The entire
Biblical account of the Flood is absurd if read in a
local-flood context. For example, there was obviously no
need for any kind of an ark if the flood were only a local
flood. Yet the Bible describes it as a huge vessel with a
volumetric capacity which can be shown to be equal to
that of over 500 standard railroad stock cars! According to
the account, the ark floated freely over all the high
mountains and finally came to rest, five months later, on
the mountains of Ararat. The highest of these mountains
today is 17,000 feet in elevation, and a flood which could
cover such a mountain six months or more was no local
flood!

Furthermore, God's promise never to send such a flood
again, sealed with the continuing testimony of the
rainbow, has been broken again and again if the Flood was
only a local flood.

A list of 96 reasons why the Flood must be understood
as worldwide is given in one of the writer's books.[4]

The tranquil-flood theory is even more ridiculous. It is
difficult to believe anyone could take it seriously and yet a
number of modern evangelical geologists do believe in this
idea. Even local floods are violent phenomena and

uniformitarian geologists today believe they are responsible for most of the geologic deposits of the earth's crust. A universal Flood that could come and go softly, leaving no geologic evidence of its passage, would require an extensive complex of miracles for its accomplishment. Anyone with the slightest understanding of the hydraulics of moving water and the hydrodynamic forces associated with it would know that a worldwide "tranquil" flood is about as reasonable a concept as a tranquil explosion!

As far as science is concerned, it should be remembered that events of the past are not reproducible, and are, therefore, inaccessible to the scientific method. Neither uniformitarianism nor catastrophism can actually be *proved* scientifically. Nevertheless, the Flood model fits all the geologic facts more directly and simply, with a smaller number of qualifications and secondary assumptions, then does the uniformitarian model.

An obvious indication of global water activity is the very existence of sedimentary rocks all over the world which, by definition, were formed by the erosion, transportation, and deposition of sediments by moving water, with the sediments gradually converted into stone after they had been deposited.

Similarly, an obvious indicator of catastrophism is the existence of fossils in the sedimentary rocks. The depositional processes must have been rapid, or fossils could not have been preserved in them.

"To become fossilized, a plant or animal must usually have hard parts, such as bone, shell, or wood. It must be buried quickly to prevent decay and must be undisturbed throughout the long process."[5]

The importance of this fact is obvious when one realizes that the identification of the geologic "age" of any given sedimentary rock depends solely upon the assemblage of fossils which it contains. The age does not depend on radiometric dating, as is obvious from the fact that the geologic age system had been completely worked out and most major formations dated before radioactivity was even discovered. Neither does the age depend upon the

152

mineralogic or petrologic character of a rock, as is obvious from the fact that rocks of all types of composition, structure, and degree of hardness can be found in any "age". It does not depend upon vertical position in the local geologic strata, since rocks of any "age" may and do rest horizontally and conformably on rocks of any other age. No, a rock is dated *solely* by its fossils.

"The only chronometric scale applicable in geologic history for the stratigraphic classification of rocks and for dating geologic events exactly is furnished by the fossils. Owing to the irreversibility of evolution, they offer an unambiguous time-scale for relative age determinations and for worldwide correlations of rocks."[6]

Thus, the existence and identification of distinctive geologic ages is based on fossils in the sedimentary rocks. On the other hand, the very existence of fossils in sedimentary rocks is *prima facie* evidence that each such fossiliferous rock was formed by aquaeous catastrophism. The one question, therefore, is whether the rocks were formed by a great multiplicity of local catastrophes scattered through many ages, or by a great complex of local catastrophes all conjoined contemporaneously in one single age, terminated by the cataclysm.

The latter is the most likely. Each distinctive stratum was laid down quickly, since it obviously represents a uniform set of water flow conditions, and such uniformity never persists very long. Each set of strata in a given formation must also have been deposited in rapid succession, or there would be evidence of unconformities — that is, periods of uplift and erosion — at the various interfaces.

Where unconformities do exist, say at the top of a formation, there may well have been an interval of uplift or tilting, at that location, followed by either sub-aerial or sub-marine erosion for a time. However, since such formations invariably grade laterally into other formations (no unconformity is worldwide), sooner or later one will

153

come to a location where there is a conformable relationship between this formation and the one above it. Thus, each formation is succeeded somewhere by another one which was deposited rapidly after the first one . . . and so on, throughout the entire geologic column.

Thus, there is no room anywhere for long ages. Each formation must have been produced rapidly, as evidenced by both its fossils and its depositional characteristics, and each formation must have been followed rapidly by another one, which was also formed rapidly! The whole sequence, therefore, must have been formed rapidly, exactly as the Flood model postulates.

But, then, what about the geologic ages? Remember that the only means of identifying these ages is by fossils and fossils speak of rapid formation. Even assuming a very slow formation of these beds, however, how can fossils tell the age of a rock?

Obviously, fossils could be distinctive time-markers only if the various kinds each had lived in different ages. But how can we know which fossils lived in which ages? No scientists were there to observe them, and true *science* requires *observation*. Furthermore, by analogy with the present (and uniformitarianism is supposed to be able to decipher the past in terms of the present), many different kinds of plants and animals are living in the present world, including even the "primitive" one-celled organisms with which evolution is supposed to have begun. Why, therefore, isn't it better to assume that all major kinds also lived together in past ages as well? Some kinds, such as the dinosaurs, have become extinct, but practically all present-day kinds of organisms are also found in the fossil world.

The only reason for thinking that different fossils should represent different ages is the assumption of evolution. If evolution is really true, then of course fossils should provide an excellent means for identifying the various ages, an "unambiguous time-scale", as Schindewolf put it. Hedberg says:

"Fossils have furnished, through their record of the

evolution of life on this planet, an amazingly effective key to the relative positioning of strata in widely-separated regions." [7]

The use of fossils as time-markers thus depends completely on "their record of evolution". But, then, how do we know that evolution is true? Why, because of the fossil record!

"Fossils provide the only historical, documentary evidence that life has evolved from simpler to more and more complex forms." [8]

So, the only proof of evolution is based on the assumption of evolution! The system of evolution arranges the fossils, the fossils date the rocks, and the resulting system of fossil-dated rocks proves evolution. Around and around we go.

How much more simple and direct it would be to explain the fossil-bearing rocks as the record in stone of the destruction of the antediluvian world by the great Flood. The various fossil assemblages represent, not evolutionary stages developing over many ages, but rather ecological habitats in various parts of the world in one age. Fossils of simple marine invertebrate animals are normally found at the lowest elevations in the geologic strata for the simple reason that they live at the lowest elevations. Fossils of birds and mammals are found only at the higher elevations because they live at higher elevations and also because they are more mobile and could escape burial longer. Human fossils are extremely rare because men would only very rarely be trapped and buried in flood sediments at all, because of their high mobility. The sediments of the "ice-age" at the highest levels are explained in terms of the drastically changed climates caused by the Flood.

The flood theory of geology,[9] which was so obvious and persuasive to the founders of geology, is thus once again beginning to be recognized as the only theory which is fully consistent with the actual *facts* of geology, as well as with the testimony of Scripture.

References

1. Stephen Jay Gould: "Is Uniformitarianism Necessary?" *American Journal of Science*, Vol. 263, (March 1965), p. 227.
2. Edgar B. Heylmun: "Should We Teach Uniformitarianism?", *Journal of Geological Education*. Vol. 19, January 1971, p. 35.
3. David Jorafsky: *Soviet Marxism and Natural Science* (New York, Columbia University Press, 1961), p. 12.
4. Henry M. Morris: *The Remarkable Birth of Planet Earth* (San Diego, Institute of Creation Research, 1972) pp. 114.
5. F.H.T. Rhodes, H.S. Zimm and P.R. Shaffer: *Fossils* (New York, Golden Press, 1962), p. 10.
6. O.H. Schindewolf: "Comments on Some Stratigraphic Terms", *American Journal of Science*, Vol. 255, June 1957, p. 394.
7. H.D. Hedberg: "The Stratigraphic Panorama", *Bulletin of the Geological Society of America*, Vol. 72, April 1961, pp. 499-518.
8. C.O. Dunbar: *Historical Geology* (New York, Wiley, 1960), p. 47.
9. See *The Genesis Flood*, by John C. Whitcomb and Henry M. Morris (Nutley, N.J., Presbyterian and Reformed, 1961), for a much more extensive treatment of the various topics discussed in this brief paper. Available also through the Institute for Creation Research, 2716 Madison Avenue, San Diego, California, 92116.

EVOLUTION AND MODERN RACISM

Henry M. Morris, Ph.D.

The Bible and Racial Origins

Some people today, especially those of anti-Christian opinions, have the mistaken notion that the Bible prescribes permanent racial divisions among men and is, therefore, the cause of modern racial hatreds. As a matter of fact, the Bible says nothing whatever about race. Neither the word nor the concept of different "races" is found in the Bible at all. As far as one can learn from a study of Scripture, the writers of the Bible did not even know there were distinct races of men, in the sense of black and yellow and white races, or Caucasian and Mongol and Negroid races, or any other such divisions.

The Biblical divisions among men are those of "tongues, families, nations, and lands" (Genesis 10:5,20,31) rather than races. The vision of the redeemed saints in heaven (Revelation 7:9) is one of "all nations, and kindreds, and people, and tongues", but no mention is made of "races". The formation of the original divisions, after the Flood, was based on different languages (Genesis 11:6-9), supernaturally imposed by God, but nothing is said about any other physical differences.

Some have interpreted the Noahic prophecy concerning his three sons (Genesis 9:25-27) to refer to three races, Hamitic, Semitic and Japhetic, but such a meaning is in no way evident from the words of this passage. The prophecy applies to the descendants of Noah's sons, and the various nations to be formed from them, but nothing is said about three races. Modern anthropologists and historians employ a much-different terminology than this simple trifurcation for what they consider to be the various races among men.

Therefore, the origin of the concept of "race" must be sought elsewhere than in the Bible. If certain Christian writers have interpreted the Bible in a racist framework, the error is in the interpretation, not in the Bible itself. In the Bible, there is only one race — the *human* race! "(God) hath made of *one*, all nations of men" (Acts 17:26).

What Is a Race?

In modern terminology, a race of men may involve quite a large number of individual national and language groups. It is, therefore, a much broader generic concept than any of the Biblical divisions. In the terminology of biological taxonomy, it is roughly the same as a "variety", or a "sub-species". Biologists, of course, use the term to apply to sub-species of animals, as well as men.

For example, Charles Darwin selected as the sub-title for his book *Origin of Species* the phrase *"The Preservation of Favoured Races in the Struggle for Life"*. It is clear from the context that he had races of animals primarily in mind, but at the same time it is also clear, as we shall see, that he thought of races of men in the same way.

That this concept is still held today is evident from the following words of leading modern evolutionist George Gaylord Simpson:

"Races of man have, or perhaps one should say 'had', exactly the same biological significance as the subspecies of other species of mammals."[1]

It is clear, therefore, that a race is not a Biblical category, but rather is a category of evolutionary biology. Each race is a sub-species, with a long evolutionary history of its own, in the process of evolving gradually into a distinct species.

As applied to man, this concept, of course, suggests that each of the various races of men is very different, though still inter-fertile, from all of the others. If they continue to be segregated, each will continue to compete as best it can with the other races in the struggle for existence and finally the fittest will survive. Or else, perhaps, they will gradually become so different from each other as to assume the character of separate species altogether (just as apes and men supposedly diverged from a common ancestor early in the so-called Tertiary Period).

Many modern biologists today would express these concepts somewhat differently than as above, and they undoubtedly would disavow the racist connotations. Nevertheless, this was certainly the point-of-view of the 19th century evolutionists, and it is difficult to interpret modern evolutionary theory, the so-called neo-Darwinian synthesis, much differently.

Nineteenth-Century Evolutionary Racism

The rise of modern evolutionary theory took place mostly in Europe, especially England and Germany. Europeans, along with their American cousins, were then leading the world in industrial and military expansion, and were, therefore, inclined to think of themselves as somehow superior to the other nations of the world. This opinion was tremendously encouraged by the concurrent rise of Darwinian evolutionism and its simplistic approach to the idea of struggle between natural races, with the strongest surviving and thus contributing to the advance of evolution.

As the 19th century scientists were converted to evolution, they were thus also convinced of racism. They were certain that the white race was superior to other races, and the reason for this superiority was to be found in Darwinian theory. The white race had advanced farther up the evolutionary ladder and, therefore, was destined either to eliminate the other races in the struggle for existence or else to have to assume the "white man's burden" and to care for those inferior races that were incompetent to survive otherwise.

Charles Darwin himself, though strongly opposed to slavery on moral grounds, was convinced of white racial superiority. He wrote on one occasion as follows:

"I could show fight on natural selection having done and doing more for the progress of civilization than you seem inclined to admit . . . The more civilized so-called Caucasian races have beaten the Turkish hollow in the struggle for existence. Looking to the world at no very distant date, what an endless number of the lower races will have been eliminated by the higher civilized races throughout the world."[2]

The man more responsible than any other for the widespread acceptance of evolution in the 19th century was Thomas Huxley. Soon after the American Civil War, in which the negro slaves were freed, he wrote as follows:

"No rational man, cognizant of the facts, believes that the average negro is the equal, still less the superior, of the white man. And if this be true, it is simply incredible that, when all his disabilities are removed, and our prognathous relative has a fair field and no favour, as well as no oppressor, he will be able to compete successfully with his bigger-brained and smaller-jawed rival, in a contest which is to be carried out by thoughts and not by bites."[3]

Racist sentiments such as these were held by all the 19th century evolutionists. A recent book[4] has documented this fact beyond any question. In a review of this book, a recent writer says:

"*Ab initio*, Afro-Americans were viewed by these intellectuals as being in certain ways unredeemably, unchangeably, irrevocably inferior."[5]

A reviewer in another scientific journal says:

"After 1859, the evolutionary schema raised additional questions, particularly whether or not Afro-Americans could survive competition with their white near-relations. The momentous answer was a resounding no . . . The African was inferior — he represented the missing link between ape and Teuton."[6]

The Modern Harvest

In a day and age which practically worshipped at the shrine of scientific progress, as was true especially during the century from 1860 to 1960, such universal scientific racism was bound to have repercussions in the political and social realms. The seeds of evolutionary racism came to fullest fruition in the form of National Socialism in Germany. The philosopher Friedrich Nietzsche, a contemporary of Charles Darwin and an ardent evolutionist, popularized in Germany his concept of the superman, and then the master race. The ultimate outcome was

Hitler, who elevated this philosophy to the status of a national policy.

> "From the 'Preservation of Favoured Races in the Struggle for Life' (i.e., Darwin's subtitle to *Origin of Species*) it was a short step to the preservation of favoured individuals, classes or nations — and from their preservation to their glorification . . . Thus it has become a portmanteau of nationalism, imperialism, militarism, and dictatorship, of the cults of the hero, the superman, and the master race . . . recent expressions of this philosophy, such as *Mein Kampf*, are, unhappily, too familiar to require exposition here."[7]

However one may react morally against Hitler, he was certainly a consistent evolutionist. Sir Arthur Keith, one of the leading evolutionary anthropologists of our century, said:

> "The German Fuhrer . . . has consciously sought to make the practice of Germany conform to the theory of evolution."[8]

With respect to the question of race struggle, as exemplified especially in Germany, Sir Arthur also observed:

> "Christianity makes no distinction of race or of colour; it seeks to break down all racial barriers. In this respect, the hand of Christianity is against that of Nature, for are not the races of mankind the evolutionary harvest which Nature has toiled through long ages to produce?"[9]

In recent decades, the cause of racial liberation has made racism unpopular with intellectuals and only a few evolutionary scientists still openly espouse the idea of a long-term polyphyletic origin of the different races.[10] On the other hand, in very recent years, the pendulum has swung, and now we have highly vocal advocates of "black power" and "red power" and "yellow power", and these advocates are all doctrinaire evolutionists, who believe their own respective "races" are the fittest to survive in man's continuing struggle for existence.

The Creationist Position

According to the Biblical record of history, the Creator's divisions among men are linguistic and national divisions, not racial. Each nation has a distinct purpose and function in the corporate life of mankind, in the divine Plan (as, for that matter, does each individual).

"(God) hath made of one, all nations of men for to dwell on all the face of the earth, and hath determined the times before appointed, and the bounds of their habitation; That they should seek the Lord, if haply they might feel after Him, and find Him (Acts 17:26,27)."

No one nation is "better" than another, except in the sense of the blessings it has received from the Creator, perhaps in measure of its obedience to His Word and fulfillment of its calling. Such blessings are not an occasion for pride, but for gratitude.

References

1. George Gaylord Simpson: "The Biological Nature of Man, *Science*, Vol. 152, April 22, 1966, p.474.
2. Charles Darwin: *Life and Letters*, 1, letter to Graham July 3, 1881, p. 316; cited in *Darwin and the Darwinian Revolution*, by Gertrude Himmelfarb (London, Chatto and Windus, 1959), p. 343.
3. Thomas Huxley: *Lay Sermons, Addresses and Reviews* (New York, Appleton, 1871), p. 20.
4. John S. Haller, Jr.: *Outcasts from Evolution: Scientific Attitudes of Racial Inferiority, 1859-1900* (Urbana, University of Illinois Press, 1971), pp. 228.
5. Sidney W. Mintz: *American Scientist*, Vol. 60, May-June 1972, p. 387.
6. John C. Burnham, *Science*, Vol. 175, February 4, 1972, p. 506.
7. Gertrude Himmelfarb, *op cit*, pp. 343-344.
8. Arthur Keith: Evolution and Ethics (New York, G.P. Putnam's Sons, 1949), p. 230.
9. *Ibid*, p. 72.

10. One notable exception, among others, is the leading anthropologist Carleton Coon. See *The Origin of Races* (New York, Alfred Knopf, 1962), pp. 724.

EVOLUTION: THE OCEAN SAYS NO!
Stuart E. Nevins, M.S.

The subject of the age of the earth and the age of the world ocean is a matter of extreme importance, If there is evidence for an old ocean, then this could be used to support the evolutionist's supposition that life arose from primitive, inorganic marine chemicals over a billion years ago. If, however, the world ocean can be shown to be a relatively youthful feature, then the evolutionist would seem to lose his case by default.

Ocean Models

Two basic models for the world ocean can be imagined. According to evolutionary-uniformitarian geologists, the earth is approximately 4.5 billion years old. The world ocean is supposed to have formed by outgassing of water by volcanic processes early in the earth's history. By no later than 1 billion years ago, in the popular scheme, the ocean reached its present size and chemical condition, and primitive one-celled life forms had already evolved by chance processes from lifeless chemicals. For a period of at least 1 billion years the ocean has remained at roughly constant salinity while the single-celled creatures evolved into mollusks, fish, reptiles, mammals, and finally man. During this vast period of time the continents have been eroding more or less continuously with debris being steadily deposited as sediments on the ocean floor.

An alternate to the evolutionist's view of the ocean is the creationist's view. According to the creationist, the ocean formed very recently — perhaps only 10,000 years ago. The earth in its original condition was covered with water (Genesis 1:2), but later God formed the ocean basins by gathering the waters together allowing the dry land to appear (Genesis 1:9). The ocean again covered the earth during the universal Flood in the days of Noah, and returned to their present basins following the Flood.

The purpose of this paper is to examine erosion and sedimentation rates to see who has the better model for the world ocean.

Ocean Sediments

The floor of the ocean is blanketed by a layer of poorly consolidated material called sediment. Small rock particles, and precipitated chemicals derived from the continents, especially by streams, form the bulk of this sediment. Chemically precipitated calcareous ooze is the most common deep ocean sediment, while continent-derived sand and mud is most common in the shallower ocean and nearer to shore.

Deep sea drilling and seismic surveys have provided much information about the thickness of sediments in the ocean. These data were quite surprising to early oceanographers who, assuming a great age for the ocean, expected a great thickness of sediment. The average thickness of deep ocean sediments is less than 0.40 mile (2100 feet). Greater thicknesses of sediments are encountered on the continental shelves and slopes. The best world average sediment thickness over the entire ocean (shallow and deep) would be about 0.56 mile or 2,950 feet.[1] This estimate is generous and would be accepted as approximately correct by most evolutionary-uniformitarian geologists.

We can now calculate the volume of ocean sediments simply by multiplying the average thickness (0.56 mile) by the area of the world ocean (139.4 million square miles).[2] The calculation shows that 77 million cubic miles of sediment are present on the ocean floor.

Next, we can estimate the mass of ocean sediments by multiplying the volume of sediments (77 million cubic miles) by the average sediment density (10.7 billion tons/cubic mile = 2.30 grams/cubic centimeter).[3] It will be discovered that the mass of ocean sediments is about 820 million billion tons.

The present topographic continents above sea level have a volume of about 30.4 million cubic miles and a mass of about 383 million billion tons. If the present continents were eroded to sea level, about 383 million billion tons of sediment would be deposited on the ocean floor. This mass is a little less than half the mass of sediment present in today's ocean. Stated another way, it would only take the erosion of twice our present continental mass to produce today's mass of ocean sediments!

Rates Of Erosion

Careful study of modern rivers on a world-wide scale shows that vast quantities of rock are being transported to the ocean. Suspended sediment, small rock particles which are carried along by river turbulence, comprise the bulk of sediment added to the ocean. The best estimate from river data suggests that 20.2 billion tons of suspended sediment enter the ocean each year.[4]

Rivers also carry dissolved chemical substances into the ocean. The chemicals are mostly bicarbonate, silica, and salts which comprise about 4.6 billion tons of sediment added to the ocean each year.[5]

Glaciers at higher latitudes are presently breaking apart and adding icebergs to the ocean. When the ice melts the entrapped sediments are deposited on the sea floor. Ice appears to be delivering about 2.2 billion tons of sediment to the ocean each year.[6]

Although little is known about the migration of fluids at great depths in the earth, water is presently being added to the oceans through the sea floor from the continents and from springs and volcanoes on the sea floor. This water also contains dissolved chemicals. A conservative estimate suggests that 0.47 billion tons of sediment are added to the ocean each year by ground waters.[7]

The seashore is constantly being worn by waves which deliver sediment to the sea. A good estimate suggests that marine erosion adds 0.28 billion tons of sediment annually.[8]

Wind-blown dust especially from desert areas and dust from volcanoes finds its way to the sea. About 0.06 billion tons go into the ocean each year.[9]

Evaporation and wind remove a small amount of salts from the ocean and deposit these on the land. The amount of sediment removed in this salt spray process as aerosols is estimated at 0.29 billion tons each year.[10]

Now that we have examined the processes which deliver and remove sediment from the ocean, we are ready to calculate the total amount of sediment going into the world ocean each year. The addition of the previous erosion estimates gives a total sediment input to the ocean of 27.5 billion tons every year. This is an enormous quantity of sediment! Most evolutionary-uniformitarian geologists would admit that this total is approximately correct.

For the sake of illustration, imagine that all of this yearly sediment were loaded into railroad freight cars each having a capacity of 11 tons. We would need 2.5 billion train cars! This is a train which would extend to the moon and back 34 times! If this train were traveling past you at 60 miles per hour, it would take 32 years to pass. The sediment total shows that 80 train cars of sediment per second are being added to the ocean!

How long would it take to deliver the present continents to the ocean if the present rate of erosion continues? There are about 30.4 million cubic miles of continental crust above sea level with a mass of 383 million billion tons. To calculate the amount of time required to deliver the present continents to the ocean we need only divide the mass of continents above sea level by the annual rate of erosion. The calculation would be:

$$\frac{383 \text{ million billion tons}}{27.5 \text{ billion tons per year}} = 14 \text{ million years}$$

The continents are being denuded at a rate that could level them in a mere 14 million years! Yet, evolutionary-uniformitarian geologists feel certain that the continents have existed for at least 1 billion years. During this supposed interval of time the present continents could have been eroded over 70 times! Yet — miracle of miracles — the continents are still here and do not appear to have been eroded even *one* time!

SEDIMENT TRANSPORTATION
PROCESS

AMOUNT OF SEDIMENT TRANSPORTED
(BILLIONS OF TONS PER YEAR)

Suspended sediment in rivers	+20.2
Dissolved chemicals in rivers	+ 4.6
Ice	+ 2.2
Ground water	+0.47
Marine erosion	+0.28
Wind-blown dust	+0.06
Salt spray	−0.29
TOTAL SEDIMENT TO OCEAN	+27.5 Billion tons per year

TABLE 1:
SEDIMENT BUDGET OF THE WORLD OCEAN

Age Of The Ocean

Even though the continents could be eroded and transported to the ocean in just 14 million years, assume that some mysterious uplifting process continues to raise the continents as they are eroding. How much sediment would form at present rates of erosion in one billion years? The answer is found by multiplying the annual rate of addition of sediments to the ocean (27.5 billion tons per year) by the alleged evolutionary age of the ocean (1 billion years). During 1 billion years 27.5 billion billion tons of sediment would be produced. This is enough to cover the entire ocean floor with 97,500 feet (18.5 miles) of sediment! In order to produce this colossal quantity of sediment an incredible layer of rock 200,000 feet (38 miles) thick would have to be eroded off of the continents. Thus, if we assume the present rate of erosion and exposed continental volumes to have existed over the evolutionist's supposed 1 billion year history of the world ocean, *we would expect a staggering layer of sediment almost 100,000 feet thick to cover the sea floor today!* Since such a monumental layer does not exist, it seems that evolutionists have grossly overestimated the age of the world ocean.

Another question is in order. How long would it take to deposit the present thickness of sediments on the ocean floor assuming constant rate of erosion? To obtain the answer we must divide the mass of sediment in the ocean by the yearly rate of sediment input. The calculation is:

$$\frac{820 \text{ million billion tons}}{27.5 \text{ billion tons per year}} = 30 \text{ million years}$$

In only 30 million years *assuming constant rate of erosion* all the ocean sediments could have accumulated. This age does not square with the over 1 billion year age assumed by evolutionary-uniformitarian geologists.

It is important to note that according to evolutionary-uniformitarian geologists the last 30 million years were the time of considerable continental denudation. The greatly accelerated erosion rates of the late Cenozoic were climaxed by the ice age, "a time when the weather went wild."[11] Modern river floodplains show evidence that vast quantities of water once passed into the ocean, exceeding modern river discharges. Scientists who have been working in deep sea drilling of sediments were recently surprised how far back the evidences of glaciation and more humid climate go into the sedimentary record. Therefore, the assumption of constant rate of sedimentation is not valid but requires greatly increased erosion rates in the past. This increased rate of sediment input to the ocean might *decrease* the apparent age of ocean sediments calculated above by a factor of ten to a hundred making it even harder to reconcile with the evolutionary model.

While the difficulties encountered with the evolutionary model are readily apparent, the creation model is consistent with the evidence. According to the creation model, the ocean reached its present condition only after the Noachian Flood. Some of the oldest ocean sediments appear to have been deposited rapidly from debris-laden water immediately after the Flood. These sedimentary layers do not require an associated long history of continental erosion.

The most recent ocean sediments appear to have been deposited in the centuries after the Flood when the climate was quite humid and when rates of erosion were significantly greater than at present. Most of the recent ocean sediments are probably not derived from erosion of continental granite, but derived from sedimentary rocks. Thus, the more recent ocean sediments appear to be chiefly "recycled" and do not require a long history. It is eminently reasonable to believe in a young ocean with an age of 10,000 years or less.

The Evolutionist's Dilemma

If the world ocean is a billion years old, there should be an enormous quantity of ocean sediments. Yet, even the evolutionist is aware of the scarcity of sediments. What would be his rebuttal to the arguments presented so far?

In order to have an ocean over a billion years old yet possessing a meager carpet of sediments, the evolutionist *must* have some process which constantly removes sediments from the sea floor. The first process which comes to mind is removing sediment by uplifting sea floor and returning ocean sediments back to the continents. This may account for a little ocean sediment loss, but the total amount of sediments on the continents is about equal to the amount on the ocean floor. Adding all the sediments on the present continents to those in the modern ocean would still be far short of the anticipated 100,000 feet of ocean sediments which should exist if the ocean is a billion years old. This process does not solve the evolutionist's dilemma.

The second process is very ingenious. If the major quantity of sediment is not being removed from the ocean by uplifting, then the evolutionist must suppose some process which plunges deep ocean sediments into the depths of the earth! The favorite method is called "sea floor spreading," and suggests that the ocean floor is like a conveyor belt. Ocean crust is assumed to form continuously at the mid ocean ridges, then it accumulates sediments as it slowly moves away from the ridge, and finally both crust and sediments are destroyed by remelting when dragged below ocean trenches. The best estimates by evolutionary-uniformitarian geologists suggest that about 2.75 billion tons of sediment per year are being destroyed by sea floor spreading. This rate is only one tenth of the modern rate of addition of sediments to the ocean. Stated another way, ocean sediments are forming today at a rate ten times faster than they are being destroyed by sea floor spreading! Thus, sea floor spreading is not able to destroy sediments fast enough.

After careful analysis of the erosion of continents and associated sedimentation in the world ocean, we must ask two urgent questions. Where is all the sediment if, as the evolutionist assumes, the ocean is over 1 billion years old? Who has the better model for the ocean — the evolutionist or the creationist? We feel confident that the true answers concerning the origin of the ocean are presented in Scripture. "The sea is His and He made it" (Psalm 95:5).

References

1. In my estimate of world average sediment thickness I have used the most recent data of M. Ewing, G. Carpenter, C. Windisch and J. Ewing: "Sediment Distribution in the Oceans: The Atlantic," *Geological Society of America Bulletin*, Vol. 84, January 1973, p. 83. Correction was made for Pacific Ocean sediments which are not as thick on the average as Atlantic Ocean sediments.
2. John N. Holeman: "The Sediment Yield of Major Rivers of the World," *Water Resources Research*, Vol. 4, August 1968, p. 737.
3. The density of deep sea sediments according to several authorities averages about 2.3 grams per cubic centimeter.
4. Robert M. Garrels and Fred T. MacKenzie: *Evolution of Sedimentary Rocks*, W.W. Norton & Co., New York, 1971, pp. 104-106.

5. *Ibid.*, pp. 102, 103.
6. *Ibid.*, p.110.
7. *Ibid.*, pp. 103, 104.
8. *Ibid.*, pp. 110, 111.
9. *Ibid.*, p. 111.
10. *Ibid.*, p. 108.
11. See the excellent discussion of late Cenozoic erosion by R.W. Fairbridge: "Denudation," in *The Encyclopedia of Geomorphology*, Reinhold Book Co., New York, 1968, pp. 261-271.
12. Y. Li: "Geochemical Mass Balance among Lithosphere, Hydrosphere, and Atmosphere," *American Journal of Science*, Vol. 272, February 1972, p. 133.

21 SCIENTISTS WHO BELIEVE IN CREATION

Young people are often taught that all scientists believe in evolution. Such a statement is, of course, quite false. There are today certainly hundreds, probably thousands, of creationist scientists.

Among the finest of such Bible — believing scientists are those that comprise the scientific staff of Christian Heritage College and the Technical Advisory Board of the Institute for Creation Research. Each of these men is not only a strong believer in special creation, a young earth, and the world-wide flood, but is also a committed Christian, strong in his knowledge of Scripture, active in his local church, and effective in his personal witness, both to salvation through Jesus Christ and to the truth of Biblical creationism. Both for information about *ICR-CHC* personnel, and for encouragement to everyone interested in these vital questions, a brief sketch of each of these men is given below.

ICR Technical Advisory Board

Physicist. **Dr. Thomas G. Barnes** is Professor of Physics at the University of Texas in El Paso. For many years he was Director of the Schellenger Research Laboratories there, in charge of numerous important governmentally-sponsored research projects in atmospheric physics. He is author of an important textbook, *Foundations of Electricity and Magnetism* (D.C. Heath Co., 1965), as well as many scientific journal articles. He is President of the Creation Research Society and is author of the recent ICR Technical Monograph, *Origin and Destiny of the Earth's*

Magnetic Field. Dr. Barnes is a deacon and teacher in El Paso's First Baptist Church and has an outstanding testimony among students and faculty on the UTEP campus.

"As a scientist my concern about evolution is that it is a barrier to scientific progress. For example, the rapid decay in the earth's magnet, a loss of 5.5×10 ampere meter^2 since first measured in 1835, is the most remarkable world-wide geophysical phenomenon ever documented. When examined in the light of electromagnetic theory and the time factor involved, this is excellent support for Special Creation. I have never seen an evolutionist who was willing to face up to this fact."

Aerospace Scientist. **Dr. Edward Blick** is Professor of Aerospace, Mechanical, and Nuclear Engineering and formerly Associate Dean of Engineering at the University of Oklahoma. He is active in aerodynamics and biomechanics research, has published many papers in this field, and is a very popular teacher at the University. He is co-author of the textbook, *Fluid Mechanics and Heat Transfer* (Addison-Wesley, 1969).

"Evolution is a scientific fairytale just as the 'flat-earth theory' was in the 12th century. Evolution directly contradicts the Second Law of Thermodynamics, which states that unless an intelligent planner is directing a system, it will always go in the direction of disorder and deterioration. Based on simple mathematics, it is possible to show that the odds against

174

forming even the simplest protein molecule by random chance is far greater than 10^{67} to one! (one followed by 67 zeros). Evolution requires a faith that is incomprehensible! Biblical Creation is the only sensible alternative."

Engineering Administrator. **Dr. David R. Boylan** is Dean of the College of Engineering at Iowa State University, one of the nation's leading scientific and engineering institutions. His B.S. is in Chemical Engineering from the University of Kansas in 1943, and his Ph.D. from Iowa State in 1952. Prior to his present appointment, he served as Director of Iowa State's Engineering Research Institute.

Biochemist. **Larry Butler** received his Ph.D. in 1964 from U.C.L.A. and is Professor of Biochemistry at Purdue University. Prior to joining the Purdue faculty in 1966, he did postdoctoral research at U.C.L.A. and the University of Arizona and served on the faculty at Los Angeles Baptist College. He has published numerous scientific articles in his field.

"I am a creationist rather than an evolutionist because, while neither of these interpretations of the origin of living things is truly scientific in the sense of being provable by experiment, only the Creationist position is true to the Scriptures. Despite theoretical claims, no organism has been experimentally demonstrated to evolve to a 'higher,' biochemically more complex form. The evidence is more consistent with a

175

pattern of degradation to 'lower,' biochemically simpler forms, in agreement with the Biblical record and with the Second Law of Thermodynamics."

Biologist. **Kenneth B. Cumming** holds degrees from Tufts and Harvard in Biology and a Ph.D. in Ecology from Harvard University (1965). He was formerly on the faculty at Virginia Polytechnic Institute and State University as an Adjunct Professor in the Department of Forestry and Wildlife. He is now a Research Associate in the Department of Biology of the University of Wisconsin at La Crosse and Instructor in Social Science at the Western Wisconsin Technological Institute, La Crosse. His full time vocation has been as a Fishery Research Biologist.

"As an ecologist, I am concerned with management of interrelationships between organisms and their environment. These circular, cyclic, and self-regulating relationships can be either integrated or disrupted by man. Today's crises, apart from natural disasters, can be attributed rightly to humanistic mismanagement from an evolutionary perspective of man's right to exploit his surroundings. Under the creation perspective, I believe that man is to be rather a responsible caretaker of God's creation, i.e. a true environmentalist. Gen. 1:28-30; Lev. 25:23; Luke 16:1-13."

Engineering Scientist. **Dr. Malcolm Cutchins** received his Ph.D. in the field of Engineering Mechanics at the Virginia Polytechnic Institute and State University in 1967, where he had also served on the faculty. He moved to Auburn University in 1966 where he is now Associate Professor of Aerospace Engineering and has been recognized as an outstanding teacher.

"Until my late 20's I gave little thought to the evolution vs. creation question. But in my exposure to engineering mechanics in graduate school I became increasingly aware of natural laws (Newton's and Kepler's, etc.) and their proofs. Other so-called 'facts" of science not based upon natural laws, but instead, based on interpretation of measurements, process rates, etc. began to stand out in sharp contrast as being heavily influenced by bias. The One behind the laws demands our recognition, our all!"

Food Scientist. **Donald Hamann** received his Ph.D. in 1967 from Virginia Polytechnic Institute and is now Professor of Food Technology at North Carolina State University in Raleigh. He formerly served on the faculties at South Dakota State University and Virginia Tech. He has authored numerous papers and holds several patents in his field.

"I believe in special creation by the God of Scripture because the mass of scientific evidence corroborates Scripture and speaks of laws initiated by God. The first and second laws of thermodynamics testify of God's ending of His creating and His providing an energy potential to operate the universe. The tendency of the universe to die an energy death opposes evolution. A later cataclysmic act of God (evidence of the universal flood) is indicated by frozen extinct animals accompanied by tropical food where freezing occurred so rapidly that internal decomposition did not take place. Such evidence, along with the clear literal statements of Genesis, make it illogical for me to accept anything but the Genesis record of creation and the Flood."

Applied Physicist—Electromagnetics. **Dr. Charles W. Harrison, Jr.** holds five degrees in Electrical Engineering and Applied Physics, including the Ph.D. degree from Harvard University in 1954. He was formerly a faculty member at Harvard and Princeton, and for over 16 years was engaged in electromagnetics research at Sandia Laboratories. He has co-authored a textbook, *Antennas and Waves: A Modern Approach* (MIT Press, 1969). He is the author of nearly 200 published papers.

Engineer. **Dr. Harold R. Henry** is Professor and Chairman of the Department of Civil and Mining Engineering at the University of Alabama in Tuscaloosa. He has a B.S. in Civil Engineering from Georgia Institute of Technology, an M.S. in Hydraulics from the University of Iowa, and a Ph.D. in Fluid Mechanics from Columbia University. He has served on the engineering faculties at Georgia Tech, Columbia, and Michigan State.

Entomologist. **Dr. Joseph Henson** is Head of the Science Division at Bob Jones University and, with other members of his science faculty, speaks frequently at creation seminars around the country. He is also very active in Christian camping ministries. He has a B.A. from Bob Jones University, M.S. in Biology, and Ph.D. in Entomology (1967) from Clemson University.

"I trusted the Lord as my Savior in a summer camp when I was 8 years old and have been privileged to love and serve Him for the ensuing 33 years. Throughout my experience in industry and research which has included work at the Chemical Corps Research and Development Center at Edgewood, Maryland, the Quartermaster Research and Development Center at Fort Lee, Virginia, and work in the analytical and metallurgical laboratories for the Vanadium Corporation of America in Durango, Colorado, and White Canyon, Utah. I have never discovered a single fact which demands an evolutionary interpretation nor have I discovered a single fact which is contrary to God's Revealed Word."

Physiologist. **Dr. John R. Meyer** is Assistant Professor of Physiology and Biophysics at the University of Louisville Medical School. He has degrees in Bible and Chemistry, and received his Ph.D. in Zoology from the State University of Iowa in 1969. He served four years as a Post-doctoral Research Fellow at the University of Colorado, in the Cardiovascular Pulmonary Research Laboratory in Denver.

Science Educator. **John N Moore** is widely known as a creationist speaker and has an outspoken and effective testimony on the campus at Michigan State University, where he is Professor of Natural Science. He is Managing Editor of the Creation Research Society Quarterly, was Co-editor of the Society's biology textbook, *Biology: A Search for Order in Complexity* (Zondervan, 1970), and is Science Editor for Zondervan Publishing House. He has the A.B. degree from Denison University and the M.S. and Ed.D. degrees from Michigan State.

"Though an evolutionist for many years, as a science teacher I restudied resource materials, and discovered that Charles Darwin actually did *not* find any conclusive evidence of change of one kind of organism into another kind. Then, after accepting Christ as my Saviour when an adult, I realized finally that all origins are completely beyond repetition, and therefore beyond any scientific study. Now I believe in Jesus Christ as the Creator of all things in contrast to belief in the totally unscientific idea of grand scale evolution and spontaneous generation of life; and, I teach that all known *scientific* data fit into the special creation account of the beginning of the universe, of life. and of man."

Theologian. **Charles C. Ryrie** has a Th.D. degree from Dallas Theological Seminary (1949) and the Ph.D. degree from the University of Edinburgh (1954). As Professor of Systematic Theology at Dallas Seminary he is one of America's top Biblical scholars. For four years he served as President of the Philadelphia College of the Bible. He has authored over fifteen important books in Biblical studies. He has also written and lectured extensively on creationism.

"To hold as I do to the principle of plain, normal interpretation of the Scriptures, I must believe in creation. All other views on this subject depart in some way from the plain meaning of the text. Since the theory of evolution is built on circular arguments, is full of gaps, and requires blind faith to believe, and since the truthfulness of creation is attested to in many parts of the Bible, as well as by Christ Himself, I can only believe in creation."

Old Testament Scholar. Best known among creationists as co-author of *The Genesis Flood,* **Dr. John C. Whitcomb, Jr.** is one of America's leading conservative Old Testament scholars. He received a B.A. from Princeton University in 1948 in the field of Ancient History, and has three degrees from Grace Theological Seminary, including the Th.D. in 1957. He now serves as Professor of Theology and Old Testament and Director of Post-Graduate Studies at Grace Seminary.

"Above and beyond all the marvelous scientific and logical evidences for a comparatively recent and supernatural origin of all things, stands the massive testimony of the written Word of God, the Bible. It was while I was an evolutionist at Princeton University in 1942/43 that God shattered my naturalistic presuppositions by means of the clear and unanswerable testimony of His own Word. Submission to the authority of the Creator Himself (see Hebrews 11:3) has provided for me an understanding of the true order, methodology, and timing of creation events that serves as the necessary foundation for all theological and scientific investigations of ultimate origins."

ICR-CHC Staff

Biochemist. **Dr. Duane T. Gish** is widely known as one of the most effective speakers and writers in the creationist movement today. He received his B.S. in Chemistry from U.C.L.A. in 1949 and his Ph.D. in Biochemistry from the University of California at Berkeley in 1953. He served on the research staff at Berkeley and at Cornell University and spent many years as research biochemist for The Upjohn Company in Kalamazoo, Michigan. He is a member of the Board of Directors of the Creation Research Society and has written many papers on creationism, as well as two ICR books *Evolution? The Fossils Say No!* and *Speculations and Experiments on the Origin of Life: A Critique.* Dr. Gish is Professor of Natural Science at Christian Heritage College and Associate Director of the Institute for Creation Research.

"I received Jesus Christ as Lord and Saviour of my life when I was about ten years of age. I have always accepted the Bible as God's unchanged and unchangeable revelation to man, and since it describes man and his universe as a special creation of God, I have always been a creationist. My university training and research experience has tremendously supported that faith, as the incredible complexity, the vast organization, the obvious plan, and evident purposefulness of every detail of the structure and function of the living cell was revealed through my biochemical studies. 'For the invisible things of Him from the creation of the world are clearly seen, being understood by the things that are made, even His eternal power and Godhead' Rom. 1:20."

Hydrologist. The Director of the Institute for Creation Research, as well as Vice-President for Academic Affairs at Christian Heritage College, is **Dr. Henry M. Morris.** Author of five books in the field of hydraulics and water resources, as well as twelve books in the field of creationism and approximately 200 articles on various subjects, Dr. Morris has been an active contributor in the study of Bible-science relationships for over 30 years. He has a B.S. from Rice University and M.S. and Ph.D. degrees from the University of Minnesota, with majors in hydraulics and minors in geology and mathematics. He spent four years in hydraulic engineering practice and then 28 years as a teacher of hydraulic engineering and hydrology in five different universities. For the period 1951-56 he was Chairman of the Civil Engineering Department at the University of Southwestern Louisiana and then from 1957 through 1970 he served as Professor of Hydraulic Engineering and Head of the Department of Civil Engineering at the Virginia Polytechnic Institute and State University. He was President of the Creation Research Society from 1967 through 1973.

"The earth's atmosphere and hydrosphere, enabling it to support a unique biosphere, provides still another evidence that the world was created by God, not evolved by chance. Furthermore, study of many of the earth's sedimentary strata in light of known principles of hydraulics shows they must have been formed rapidly and continuously in a great cataclysm. Both support the clear teaching in the Bible (note II Peter 3:5, 6) of special creation and a world-wide flood."

Geophysicist. **Harold S. Slusher** is in great demand as a speaker on creationist astronomy and geophysics. He has a B.S. degree in Mathematics from the University of Tennessee in 1954 and an M.S. in Geophysics in 1960 from the University of Oklahoma, with additional study at New Mexico State University. He has been in charge of the geophysics and astrophysics programs at the University of Texas (El Paso) for 13 years, as well as Director of the Kidd Memorial Seismic Observatory there. He is a member of the Board of Directors of the Creation Research Society and was Co-Editor of the Society's biology textbook. He is now Adjunct Professor of Planetary Science at Christian Heritage College and will assume permanent fulltime directorship of the new CHC degree program in Planetary Science in June, 1974.

Medical Scientist. **Robert H. Franks** is Professor of Biological Sciences at Christian Heritage College, teaching courses in general biology and missionary medicine. He is also a practicing physician in San Diego and is a popular Bible teacher and speaker on creationism. He received his B.A. in biology from San Diego State University in 1956 and his M.D. degree from the U.C.L.A. Medical School in 1960.

"The Bible states, 'In the beginning God created the heavens and the earth. . .' (Gen. 1:1), and that 'God created man in his own image. . .' (Gen. 1:27). My own heart says amen to this as I study the world about me and the design of the human body. Any other explanation is chaotic and does not explain the well-ordered functioning of the solar system and man's organs. 'I will praise thee: for I am fearfully and wonderfully made. . .' (Psalms 139:14)."

Chemist. **William A. Beckman** has degrees from Youngstown University and Washington State University, receiving his Ph.D. (Chemistry) from Western Reserve University in 1959. He is Professor of Physical Sciences at Christian Heritage College and is also Head of the Physical Sciences Division at Southwestern Junior College in San Diego, where he has instituted a regular course on scientific creationism, unique in secular institutions.

"When Jesus entered my heart at the age of 12, evolution was beginning to make its bid for acceptance in the minds of men, and young minds were most easily swayed. Mine was one of them. But lurking back in my thinking were many questions. Entering college and studying more intensely the facts of physics and chemistry, I found that the only way I could truly understand this present world was by the Word of God and the inspiration of the Holy Spirit."

Engineering Physicist. **Dr. Maurice Nelles** is an Adjunct Professor and Special Lecturer at Christian Heritage College, having retired from a distinguished career in education, research, and industry. He has B.S. and D.Sc. degrees from South Dakota State University and a Ph.D. from Harvard University. He has served on the faculties at South Dakota State University, Columbus University, the University of Virginia, and the University of Southern California. At U.S.C., he was first Head of its Aeronautical Engineering Department. He has served as Director of Research for the Borg-Warner Corporation and Director of Research for the Technicolor Corporation. He is author of many books and papers and has served on numerous important industrial and governmental committees. He is an excellent Bible teacher and serves on the session of La Jolla's First Presbyterian Church.

"I have been asking God's guidance for over fifty years. God prepared the way for me to obtain very broad experience in many fields of science and technology. I have never set out to prove God's Word, but I have never encountered anything to disprove it, when I knew enough. I know God can do anything at any time, and the man-made laws of science are fallible and I have observed many exceptions. I continue to believe the Bible one hundred percent, for it is true."

Geologist. **Stuart E. Nevins** is Assistant Professor of Earth Sciences at Christian Heritage, teaching courses in geology. He is also a naval officer, teaching special courses in oceanography. He has contributed several articles on flood geology to the Creation Research Society Quarterly and other publications. He has a B.S. in Geology from University of Washington and M.S. in Geology from San Jose State University.

"Our planet provides a marvelous display of God's wisdom and handiwork. The mass of the earth, distance from the sun, rotation, tilt, ratio of land to sea, and density and composition of the atmosphere are of amazing exactness to maintain life and geologic processes. The Bible accurately describes many of the earth's processes and structures without scientific blunders. For example, how did Job know about the 'springs of the sea' (Job 38:16) unless an omniscient God told him? The history of the earth described in the Bible is fully consistent with all true data of historical geology. Who can deny that there was a great, catastrophic inundation of the earth? As a geologist I must stand and marvel at the mighty testimony which God has given in the earth. Certainly, only with God is perfect wisdom. He alone has true counsel and understanding."

RECOMMENDED BOOKS
FOR FURTHER READING

Note: All books listed below may be obtained from Crea-
tion-Life Publishers, P.O. Box 15666, San Diego,
California 92115.

Books by Henry M. Morris, Ph.D.
(Director, Institute for Creation Research)

The Genesis Flood
(*co-author John C. Whitcomb, Jr., Th.D.*)
1961; 15th Printing, 1972........Cloth $6.95; Paper $3.95
The standard classic text in the field of scientific Biblical
creationism and catastrophism. Thoroughly documented
treatment of the Biblical and scientific implications of
creation and the flood.

The Twilight of Evolution
1963; 13th Printing, 1972........Cloth $2.95; Paper $1.50
Documented study of the origin and implications of evolution, with a refutation of its supposed evidences.

Biblical Cosmology and Modern Science
1970; 4th Printing, 1972....................Paper $2.50
Scientific and Biblical expositions of many aspects of cosmology, covering origins, catastrophism, eschatology,
chronology, populations analysis, sedimentary fossiliza-
tion, and thermodynamics. Includes discussion and refutation of day-age theory, gap theory, and allegorical theory.

The Bible Has The Answer
1971; 3rd Printing, 1972........Cloth $4.50; Paper $3.25
Scientific, logical and Biblical answers of 100 most frequent
questions on the Bible and science, evolution, supposed
mistakes in Scripture, difficult doctrines, social problems,
and practical Christian living. Complete topical and scripture indexes. On doctrinal questions, orientation is pre-
millennial and Baptistic; on others, non-denominational.

Science, Scripture, and Salvation
1965; Revised Ed. 1971
Biblical, scientific, and devotional exposition of the first eleven chapters of Genesis. Designed for use in Sunday Schools, but also useful for other groups and for individual study.

Junior (Grades 4, 5, & 6)	Student $0.60	Teacher $1.00
Youth (Grades 7 - 12)	Student $0.85	Teacher $1.00
Adult	Student $1.25	Teacher $1.25

The Bible and Modern Science
1957; Revised Ed. 1968......................Paper $0.50
Evangelistic presentation of evidences for the scientific validity of the Bible, including historical and prophetic confirmation. Over a quarter of a million copies in print.

Evolution and the Modern Christian
1967; 4th Printing, 1972....................Paper $1.00
Popular-level exposition of evidence for creation versus evolution. Especially written for young people.

Studies in the Bible and Science
1966; 5th Printing, 1971....................Paper $1.95
Sixteen studies on special topics, including the Bible as a scientific textbook, evidence of Christ and the Trinity in nature, Biblical hydrology, concept of power in Scripture, scientism in historical geology, and others.

The Remarkable Birth of Planet Earth
1973 ....Paper $1.50
A concise, yet comprehensive, discussion of the Biblical and theological aspects of creationism in the light of modern science.

TECHNICAL
MONOGRAPH SERIES

Speculations and Experiments Related to
The Origin of Life: A Critique
By Duane T. Gish, Ph.D.
ICR Technical Monograph No. 1
1972 . . . . .Paper $2.50
A technical monograph on the naturalistic theories of the
origin of life, documenting the biochemical impossibility
for non-living chemicals to evolve into living molecules.

Critique of Radiometric Dating
By Harold S. Slusher, M.S.
ICR Technical Monograph No. 2 . . . . Paper $2.50
A study of the principles, assumptions, and methods of the
most frequently used radioactive "clocks", including
Carbon-14, uranium-lead, thorium-lead, potassium-argon,
and rubidium-strontium. The fallacies, weaknesses, and
limitations of such methods are exposed.

Origin and Destiny of the Earth's
Magnetic Field
By Thomas G. Barnes, M.S., Sc.D.
ICR Technical Monograph No. 4 . . . . .Paper $2.50
An analysis of the nature and rate of decay of the earth's
magnetic field, yielding startling new evidence that the
earth cannot be more than about 10,000 years old. Written
to be comprehensible to both scientist and non-scientist.
Dr. Barnes is Professor of Physics at the University of
Texas, El Paso.

OTHER BOOKS

Evolution? The Fossils Say No!
By Duane T. Gish, Ph.D.
1973 Revised and enlarged edition . . . . .Paper $1.95
A brief and compelling popular summary of evidence from science, especially the fossil record, demonstrating the fallacies of evolution and the necessity of special creation.

Adventure on Ararat
By John D. Morris, B.S.
1973 . . . . .Paper $1.95
A fascinating account of the 1972 ICR expedition to Mt. Ararat in search of Noah's Ark, believed still to be preserved in a frozen lake somewhere on the high slopes of Mt. Ararat. Beautiful photographs, exciting adventure, danger, miraculous protection.

Creation: Acts • Facts • Impacts!
Ed. by Henry M. Morris, Ph.D., Duane T. Gish, Ph.D., Geo. M. Hillestad
1973 . . . . .Paper $1.95
A compilation of the "Impact Series" papers, plus all the articles of permanent interest in the first 14 issues of *ICR Acts & Facts* through December 1973. A unique book recording the continuing revival of creationism.

Scientific Creationism for Public Schools
Ed. by Henry M. Morris, Ph.D.
1974 . . . . .Cloth $5.95; Paper $3.95
A handbook for teachers, school administrators and others concerned with the scientific evidence supporting the creation model of origins as an alternative to the evolution model. The treatment is logical and scientific rather than religious, and is courteous and positive rather than critical. Scientifically documented and authoritative, but nevertheless written in a manner easily understood by those with non-scientific backgrounds. Compactly arranged for covenient reference use. Also available in Christian School edition at the same price.

Many Infallible Proofs
By Henry M. Morris, Ph.D.
A comprehensive handbook on practical Christian evidences for use either as a textbook in apologetics, as a tool in witnessing to the skeptic, or as a book for informing and strengthening one's own faith. Evidences from history, prophecy, science and common sense demonstrating Christianity and the Bible to be true. Answers to Biblical criticism, alleged contradictions, moral problems, scientific mistakes and other fallacies charged against the Christian faith.
Approximately 400 pages.
Cloth $5.95; Paper $4.95

The Early Earth
By John C. Whitcomb, Jr., Th.D.
1972 . . . . Paper $1.50
Studies in special topics relating to the Genesis record of creation, including the origin and nature of man, critical analysis of the gap theory, and others. Illustrated.

The World That Perished
By John C. Whitcomb, Jr., Th.D.
1973 . . . . Paper $1.95
This forceful sequel to the author's earlier book, *The Genesis Flood* (co-authored with Dr. Henry M. Morris, now in its sixteenth printing), restates, updates, and defends in a more popular form the basic Biblical and scientific evidence for the Genesis Flood as a global catastrophe, for which abundant evidence is still to be seen.